0073837

DATE DUE

MAR 2 1 1995	
MAY 0 3 1995	
JAN 0 2 1996	
JUN 05 1996	
NOV 2 0 1996	
MAY 2 7 1997	
JUL 1 1 1997	

BRODART   Cat. No. 23-221

NATURAL

STRESS-BUSTERS

FOR THE WHOLE FAMILY

Natural
STRESS-BUSTERS
For The Whole Family

▼ ▼ ▼ ▼

LYNN
ALLISON

COOL HAND COMMUNICATIONS, INC.

©1993 Lynn Allison
First Printing

COOL HAND COMMUNICATIONS, INC.
1098 N.W. Boca Raton Boulevard
Suite #1
Boca Raton, FL 33432

Library of Congress #93-71986
ISBN: 1-56790-099-2

Printed in the United States of America

Cover by Cheryl Nathan
Illustrations by Mark Cantrell

This book is dedicated to the late Dr. Hans Selye, the "father of stress," who taught me that self-acceptance is the first order of business if you want to take control of your life.

Contents

▼ ▼ ▼ ▼

▼ ▼ ▼

Acknowledgments

▼ ▼ ▼ ▼

I'd like to thank Dr. Joan Borysenko, for her excellent books and her personal pledge to "stop and smell the roses"; Jackie Keeley, who introduced me to the joy and serenity of Buddhism and the meaning of unconditional love; Claudia Suarez, my wise and wonderful trainer who constantly reminds me to slow down because "flowers grow in the dark"; Chris Hedrick, who operates a stress-free publishing house even in the heat of commercial combat; and of course, Pine Knot, the jolly old fellow whose simple lifestyle gives me perspective on our helter-skelter life.

▼ ▼ ▼

Introduction

▼ ▼ ▼ ▼

Stress is one of the most serious health problems of the 20th century, according to a United Nations report. It prevents us from enjoying our lives as happy, healthy, and optimistic human beings. Many people are literally crippled from effects of excess stress. They are riddled with aches and pains, suffer tortuous headaches and live under a cloud of dark pessimism and unhappiness.

Perhaps your life is plagued by stress. You feel constantly anxious and pressured with work, family, and personal problems. You secretly know there must be a better way, but you feel trapped by a world filled with too many responsibilities and not enough fun.

This book is for you and anyone else who wants to regain a sense of joy and happiness in life. It contains tried-and-true techniques to help you change your thinking from negative to positive, from gloom to optimism. You learn how to make stress work *for* you instead of against you by simply shifting your focus.

The following story demonstrates the principle of stress-busting through mind power:

▼ ▼ ▼

There were two women who had rose gardens. One would awaken every morning, look out onto her garden and groan:

"Oh, there are so many weeds in my garden. It is going to take me forever to get rid of them!"

The other woman calmly put on her gardening gloves and hummed to herself as she methodically removed the weeds surrounding her roses.

"Oh, my beautiful roses," she said. "How lovely you look and smell!"

The first woman directed her attention to the weeds instead of the roses. She focused on the negative task at hand instead of the pleasure of her roses. Therefore, her garden became a source of stress instead of a haven of joy.

The second woman, however, saw only the positive side of her garden, the delightful blooming roses. She was well aware that the weeds did exist, and that they had to be removed, but she embarked upon her task with a positive attitude. The weeds in her garden were not a source of stress. They were merely obstacles to overcome.

Stress, like those nasty weeds in the rose garden, can spring up and choke you. It can stifle your enjoyment of the good life and make you miserable. Stress can even make you sick, as many medical experts have proved time and again.

Doctors and researchers blame stress for many of the major life-threatening diseases in our society. There is mounting evidence that rampant stress due to social and financial pressures can lower your body's immune system, making it an ideal host for cancer, arthritis, diabetes, high blood pressure, ulcers, and substance abuse.

Sociologists say unchecked stress can lead to physical and domestic violence. Psychologists say stress can trigger a host of mental and emotional ailments.

Consider these frightening statistics:

- 25 million Americans suffer from high blood pressure;
- 1 million have heart attacks each year;
- 8 million have stomach ulcers;

▼ ▼ ▼

- An estimated 12 million are alcoholics;
- They fill 230 million prescriptions for tranquilizers each year.

Add to these numbers the tragic traffic accidents that result from people driving recklessly under pressure or under the influence of alcohol or drugs, and the numbers of stress-related deaths and illnesses soar even higher.

Stress is nothing new. It's not a 20th-century phenomenon that suddenly appeared to plague our lives. According to Dr. Hans Selye, the brilliant "father" of stress research, stress is an age-old mechanism. It is:

- The normal wear and tear of life;
- The result of either pleasant or unpleasant events that change our biological response;
- The trigger that can mobilize our bodies' defense systems to adapt to hostile or life-threatening events;
- Dangerous *only* when it is unduly prolonged, comes too often, or concentrates on one particular area of the body.

In other words, *stress—when kept in check and under control—can actually help propel us forward to meet new challenges.*

We all know those super-charged people who seem to face life head on. They have energy to burn. They seem to tackle each challenge in their lives with aplomb and unbridled enthusiasm.

And we know those who find even simple tasks a burden. Just getting out of bed in the morning is sometimes a monumental task for these folks.

What makes the difference? What makes one person rise above life's obstacles and another become buried in its challenges? Some say it's a matter of physical energy. To some extent, this is so. But we can also be dead tired, too tired to even move, when an exciting challenge or opportunity comes knocking at the door.

▼ ▼ ▼

Suddenly, we seem to find limitless energy. We are filled with the positive power that comes from inside. Our bodies now possess the will and ability to sail through tasks that would have seemed insurmountable a few minutes before.

This mind-body connection is so powerful that by learning how to remove negativity and *distress* from our lives, we fill ourselves with new energy, happiness and success in our endeavors.

As many wise men and women have noted, the kind of life you lead is determined by your attitude, the way you greet each day and how you handle yourself under pressure. If you choose to live stress-free, you will find that life meets you at this level.

I'm not a Ph.D. nor a certified counselor. I'm an average woman who has been the victim of physical disabilities, a devastating divorce and the loss of a child. I've been a single, working mother who's had to juggle four jobs to make ends meet, and had to deal with the trials and tribulations of raising children in a hostile environment.

Along my rocky journey, I knew deep down that there had to be a better way, a simpler way to live that involved more laughter and fewer tears; more quality time and less raucous; more meaning and less superficiality.

I discovered that stress can be a challenge rather than an obstacle; that by changing my own thinking about people, places and events, I could view them in a more positive light. I learned that by controlling my thoughts I could eliminate the harmful, destructive elements that were eating away at my well-being. By getting off the treadmill and working at my own development, I managed to turn my life around. Today I am a totally different person than the stressed-out, frenetic woman I was 20 years ago. I'm far calmer, more at peace with myself and have greater self-confidence than ever before.

By removing stress from your life, you allow your positive energy to flow freely through your body and soul. You be-

▼ ▼ ▼

come a happier person, full of joy, instead of an unhappy victim of circumstances.

No matter what your lot in life, the process of dealing with stress in a constructive manner can—and will—change your life around. If you are caught in the web of negative thinking, depression and unhappiness, now is the time to break away. Eliminate stress from your life and take control of your destiny. You have nothing to lose and a lifetime of peace and pleasure to gain.

What Is Stress?

When I looked up the definition of "stress" in my Webster's dictionary, I found it interesting that the word just below stress is "stretch." While stress is defined as a "strain of force that deforms" and "a physical or mental tension," to stretch means "to reach out, extend and spread beyond normal limits."

Those who have learned that there is little coincidence in life, will not consider this fortunate progression of definitions strange.

To remove stress from your life, you must learn to stretch your mind beyond its normal limitations. This isn't a difficult chore, nor is it weird or strange.

Trained meditators can tame their bodily functions through mind power. They can lower their heart rate, reduce blood pressure, and even remove their appetite and need for food for days on end.

In our quest for progress through technology, we have forgotten how powerful the mind can be and how we can regain control over our lives by harnessing this great power. Stress can be reduced and eventually eliminated from our lives simply by changing our minds from working in a negative to a positive operational mode.

Dr. Selye made psychological history when he redefined the word stress by dividing it into two categories. He de-

▼ ▼ ▼

scribed negative stress, the kind that tears us apart and leads to illness, as *dis-stress*. The second kind of stress is purely positive. It is the life force that propels us to achieve great things.

I had the good fortune to interview Dr. Selye during his last years. At the age of 70, he was a vibrant, intelligent and humorous fellow who still had an eye for the ladies and a quick wit to boot.

"You must use stress to better your life, not destroy it," he said. "Learn from your challenges. Use obstacles as opportunities to develop your survival skills. Instead of letting adversity beat you down, find a way to overcome it."

All people have stress in their lives. Rich men have stress. Poor men have stress. Great beauties have as much stress in their lives as we ordinary folk. Just look at the tragic lives of Marilyn Monroe and Elvis Presley. You'd think these stellar personalities would have had the world by the tail, but that was not the case.

Despite the money, good looks and power, they couldn't cope with the stress in their lives, and that inability eventually led to their untimely deaths.

Most of us enviously admire so-called people of leisure who seem to have it all: money, lovely cars, beautiful homes and exotic vacations.

"How can they possibly have stress in their lives?" you ask yourself. "If I had their money, I'd be happier than heck!"

Nine times out of ten, however, their lives are no better than yours. The very wealthy worry constantly about losing their money. The very powerful are terrified that their authority might be usurped.

Their problems are as monumental to them as yours are to you. And your problems would probably seem trivial to the mother in India who must watch her child starve to death. Everything is relative. Once you learn how to put your problems into perspective, their power over you is released and you are on the road to a stress-free life.

▼ ▼ ▼

Losing money, failing and getting older or fatter are not stressful situations in themselves. It is how we regard these events that determines whether they're stressful or not.

To deal with and remove stress from your life and become the clear-thinking, open-minded, relaxed person you truly deserve to be, you must first learn how to quickly identify negative stress before it zooms out of proportion, and then deflate or redirect its energy into positive channels.

If this sounds like *Mission: Impossible*, rest assured it's not. There are many ways you can learn to deal with stress, and they are all fun and exciting methods to master. Yes, this means you'll have to practice and set aside a definite stress-busting time each day to re-learn how to unclutter your mind and heal your body from the ravages of negative stress.

As children we used to react spontaneously to events in our lives and could spend hours watching a caterpillar wiggle its way up a tree trunk. We used to indulge in Saturday morning cartoons and laugh ourselves silly over the antics of inane characters.

But through the years, the layers of social responsibility, unhealthy guilt and financial burdens enveloped the wide-eyed child we used to be. We became cocooned in stressful terms such as "should have," "could have," and "must have." We forgot how to enjoy the moment and see things from a clear-minded, unassuming perspective.

To live your life fully and happily, you must strip off the layers of shame, guilt, duality and unhappiness. Peel down to the real core of your being. Once you start operating at a level of honesty and awareness, you'll see what you previously perceived as stressful challenges from a new and positive horizon.

The time to start is now. Stop being a victim of deadly stress and break the chains once and for all. Freedom from stress will give you the inner resources you need to build a full and productive life.

▼ ▼ ▼

Chapter One

LEARNING TO IDENTIFY
STRESS

We know that stress affects everyone and that, with proper management, we can make stress work *for* rather than *against* us.

In fact, researchers at the U.S. Department of Health and Human Services in Rockville, Maryland, state that stress is actually a desirable part of our lives.

"Stress adds flavor, challenge and opportunity to life," according to a report from the department's Mental Health Administration. "Too much stress, however, can seriously affect your physical and mental well-being. A major challenge in this stress-filled world of today is to make stress work for you instead of against you."

How much stress do you have in your life? Take a moment and look over the following chart developed by Drs. T.H. Holmes and R.H. Rahe. It's called the Social Readjustment Ratings Scale and is used to loosely determine the value or level of stress in our lives.

▼ ▼ ▼

THE HOLMES-RAHE SCALE

Life Event	Lifechange Units
Death of a spouse	100
Divorce	73
Marital Separation	65
Imprisonment	63
Death of a close family member	63
Personal injury or illness	53
Marriage	50

Life Event	Lifechange Units
Dismissal from work	47
Marital reconciliation	45
Retirement	45
Change in health of a family member	44
Pregnancy	40
Sexual difficulties	39
Change in financial state	38
Number of arguments with spouse	35
Major mortgage	32
Foreclosure of mortgage or loan	30
Change in responsibilities at work	29
Son or daughter leaves home	29
Trouble with in-laws	29
Outstanding personal achievement	28
Spouse begins or stops work	26
Begin or end school	26
Change in living conditions	25
Revision of personal habits	24
Trouble with boss	23
Change in work hours or conditions	20
Change of residence	20
Change of schools	20
Change of recreation	19
Change in church activities	19

▼ ▼ ▼

Change in social activities	18
Minor mortgage or loan	17
Change in sleeping habits	16
Vacation	(13)
Christmas	12
Minor violation of the law	11

Scoring: Add up your total score. If you have accumulated more than 300 Lifechange Units in one year you are at risk for stress-related illness; 150-299 reduces the risk by 30 percent; a score of less than 150 poses only a slight chance of illness.

Remember, however, that this scale is merely an overall indicator of what may or may not trigger a stress response in your body. Some people fall ill at the slightest sign of stress, while others seem almost indestructible. They are seldom sick, always cheerful and full of energy. These people have learned how to deal with stressful events in their lives in a positive way.

HOW YOU DEAL WITH STRESS

Researchers have shown that despite individual differences, there is a common physical reaction to stress. The body responds to stress by going through three stages:

- alarm
- resistance
- exhaustion

To understand how these stages actually work, let's take the example of a typical commuter in rush-hour traffic. If a car suddenly pulls out in front of him, his initial alarm reaction may include fear of an accident, anger at the driver who committed the action and general frustration.

His body responds in the alarm stage by releasing hormones into the bloodstream which cause his face to flush, perspiration to form, his stomach to sink and his limbs to tighten.

▼ ▼ ▼

During the next stage, called resistance, his body attempts to take action and repair the damage caused by the alarm stage. If the near-accident situation goes away, his body can temporarily sink into the third stage—exhaustion—for repair.

But if the stressful environment continues to assault his body, the driver will not have time to make the necessary anti-stress repairs. If his commute is one of constant traffic jams and irate drivers, he will soon become conditioned to tighten up and grit his teeth every time he gets into the car for the ride to or from work.

Indeed, he may develop migraine headaches, stomach ulcers, backaches or other stress-related symptoms merely at the *thought* of commuting.

Similarly, a person who absolutely hates his or her job may develop insidious chronic illness with no apparent cause.

I remember a particularly stressful period in my life as I struggled to raise my two daughters when I felt constantly ill. I was a single mother, holding down three jobs and trying to play the role of supermom at the same time.

I'd rush from work to the kitchen to make dinner. After dinner I'd deal with homework, iron their uniforms for school, make lunches and try to schedule some free time for my activities.

I felt pulled and torn in a million different directions. How could I make Christina's softball practice when I was on a deadline for an article? Would I be able to talk my boss into giving me time off to attend Melina's piano recital?

My body eventually rebelled and I found myself literally living at the doctor's office with a series of complaints ranging from chronic low energy to stomach pains. Even my teeth suffered under the stress, and I had five root canals in six months!

Finally, I had to face the fact that unless I regained some control over my stress, I'd be a basket case of nerves. This led to my extensive research and self-development through a variety of stress-building readings and methods.

▼ ▼ ▼

The Chemical Connection

Scientists at Johns Hopkins University recently discovered that you can actually trace certain chemical reactions in the brain to see how an individual copes with stress.

Dr. Solomon Snyder, a neuroscientist and member of the research team, says:

"Being able to measure the reaction of stress on the body provides a powerful tool to determine how you deal with stress."

The scientists call the specific response CRF (corticotrophin releasing factor). They found that when the body is assaulted by stress, the brain releases CRF to stimulate the pituitary gland, the master gland of the body's stress system.

While these scientists plan to research how to artificially control the CRF, experts in other fields, including meditators and religious leaders, have long known that through the power of our minds we can *naturally* control our bodies' response to stress.

When I was in my stressful period, I responded by doing all the wrong things. I ignored the symptoms, which was mistake number one. I internalized the problem instead of facing it head on. I used cigarettes, alcohol and food to dull the ache within.

Eventually, I realized that I was on a dead-end road and I certainly did not want to live my life with Band-Aid therapies. So I learned to pinpoint stressful factors in my life and deal with—or eliminate—them. The methods I used for my own stress-busting can be easily mastered by anyone and applied to every stressful situation.

The Victim Complex

Many people argue that they are victims of circumstances beyond their control.

▼ ▼ ▼

"But you don't understand," counters Renee, a 46-year-old divorcee who admits she is constantly "stressed out."

This lovely and wealthy woman feels she is a prisoner, locked in the bonds of her husband's alimony and her children's demands.

"I can't work or Simon will cut off my alimony and child support," she says. "I hate getting up in the morning because there's nothing to do except make time with the children. I have breakfast, go to my exercise class and spend the rest of the day shopping or just gabbing with the girls until the kids come home from school.

"I know I occasionally eat too much and have a few too many cocktails in the evening to pass the time," Renee continues. "I'd love to change my life but I can't until the kids are grown and I have a life of my own."

Renee's story is not unique; millions of people have their lives on hold for one reason or another. They may be convinced their reasons are legitimate, but a wise observer will point out that they can take control of their lives. What a shame it is that lives are wasted on lame excuses.

Renee may appear to be trapped in a no-end situation, but you and I upon hearing her lament can easily think of several ways she can break free.

What Renee must do is take stock of her inner self as if taking an inventory of goods. What are her strengths and weaknesses? What makes her happy and what makes her upset? Living dishonestly leads to stress. Sometimes, not making a decision can cause more heartache than taking a risk and getting on with your life.

Renee could go back to school, become a volunteer or develop fulfilling hobbies. Or, if she really wants a paying job, maybe she should just forsake her alimony and strike out on her own.

We all must learn how to identify and cope with the stress in our lives and then take appropriate action.

Try the next three tests just for fun. They were provided

▼ ▼ ▼

by the National Institutes of Mental Health, and reprinted from *Controlling Stress and Tension: A Holistic Approach* by Daniel Dirdano and George Everly (Prentice-Hall). They will help you assess your particular vulnerability to stress from specific triggers.

pg 2 STRESS TEST PART ONE

Read and choose the most appropriate answer for each of the ten questions as it actually pertains to you:

1. When I can't do something "my way," I simply adjust to do it the easier way.
   A) Almost always true; B) Usually true; C) Usually false; D) Almost always false.

2. I get "upset" when someone in front of me drives slowly.
   A) Almost always true; B) Usually true; C) Usually false; D) Almost always false.

3. It bothers me when my plans are dependent upon others.
   A) Almost always true; B) Usually true; C) Usually false; D) Almost always false.

4. Whenever possible, I tend to avoid large crowds.
   A) Almost always true; B) Usually true; C) Usually false; D) Almost always false.

5. I am uncomfortable having to stand in long lines.
   A) Almost always true; B) Usually true; C) Usually false; D) Almost always false.

6. Arguments upset me.
   A) Almost always true; B) Usually true; C) Usually false; D) Almost always false.

7. When my plans don't "flow smoothly," I become anxious.
   A) Almost always true; B) Usually true; C) Usually false; D) Almost always false.

▼ ▼ ▼

8. I require a lot of room (space) in which to live and work.
   A) Almost always true; B) Usually true; C) Usually false;
   D) Almost always false.

9. When I am busy at some task, I hate to be disturbed.
   A) Almost always true; B) Usually true; C) Usually false;
   D) Almost always false.

10. I believe that "all good things are worth waiting for."
    A) Almost always true; B) Usually true; C) Usually false;
    D) Almost always false.

To score: 1 and 10 A=1pt., B=2pts., C=3pts., D=4pts. 2 through 9 A=4 pts., B=3pts., C=2pts., D=1 pt.

Scores in excess of 25 suggest your vulnerability to specific areas of stress.

The next test is a good indicator of how much we feel victimized by our lives. If you score higher than 25 points, you have a tendency to become bogged down by your responsibilities and feel overloaded most of the time. Use the appropriate chapters in this book to help you streamline and regain control over your life.

STRESS TEST PART TWO

Circle the letter of the response option that best answers the following 10 questions.

How often do you...

1. Find yourself with insufficient time to complete your work?
   A) Almost always; B) Very often; C) Seldom; D) Never.

2. Find yourself becoming confused and unable to think clearly because too many things are happening at once?
   A) Almost always; B) Very often; C) Seldom; D) Never.

▼ ▼ ▼

16

3. Wish you had help to get everything done?
   A) Almost always; B) Very often; C) Seldom; D) Never.

4. Feel your boss/professor simply expects too much from you?
   A) Almost always; B) Very often; C) Seldom; D) Never.

5. Feel your family/friends expect too much from you?
   A) Almost always; B) Very often; C) Seldom; D) Never.

6. Find your work infringing upon your leisure hours?
   A) Almost always; B) Very often; C) Seldom; D) Never.

7. Find yourself doing extra work to set an example to those around you?
   A) Almost always; B) Very often; C) Seldom; D) Never.

8. Have to skip a meal so that you can get work completed?
   A) Almost always; B) Very often; C) Seldom; D) Never.

9. Feel that you have too much responsibility?
   A) Almost always; B) Very often; C) Seldom; D) Never.

10. Find yourself losing or forgetting basic items because you can't focus on the moment?
    A) Almost always; B) Very often; C) Seldom; D) Never.

To score: A=4 pts., B=3 pts., C=2 pts., D=1 pt. Total up your score for this exercise.

This test measures your vulnerability to "overload," i.e., having too much to do. Scores in excess of 25 seem to indicate vulnerability to this source of stress.

This final assessment was created by Dr. George S. Everly of the University of Maryland. While he admits it is not a clinical tool, the test does help measure how well you are coping with the existing stress in your life. Follow the instructions for each of the 14 items listed below. When you have completed all the items, total your points and place that score in the box provided.

STRESS TEST PART THREE

_10_   1. Give yourself 10 points if you feel you have a supportive family around you.

____ 2. Give yourself 10 points if you actively pursue a hobby.

_10_   3. Give yourself 10 points if you belong to some social or activity group that meets at least once a month (other than your family).

____ 4. Give yourself 15 points if you are within five pounds of your "ideal" body weight, considering your height and bone structure.

____ 5. Give yourself 15 points if you practice some form of "deep relaxation" at least three times a week. Deep relaxation exercises include meditation, imagery, yoga, etc.

____ 6. Give yourself 5 points for each time you exercise thirty minutes or longer during the course of an average week.

_10_   7. Give yourself 5 points for each nutritionally balanced and wholesome meal you consume during the course of an average day.

____ 8. Give yourself 5 points if you do something you really enjoy which is "just for you" during the course of an average week.

____ 9. Give yourself 10 points if you have some place in your home that you can go in order to relax and/or be by yourself.

____ 10. Give yourself 10 points if you practice time-managment techniques in your daily life.

____ 11. Subtract 10 points for each pack of cigarettes you smoke during the course of an average day.

____ 12. Subtract 5 points for each evening during the course of an average week that you take any form of medication or chemical substance (including alcohol) to help you sleep.

▼ ▼ ▼

_____ 13. Subtract 10 points for each day during the course of an average week that you consume any form of medication or chemical substance (including alcohol) to reduce your anxiety or just calm you down.

_____ 14. Subtract 5 points for each evening during to course of an average week that you bring work home; work that was meant to be done at your place of employment.

Now calculate your total score and place it in the box on the left. A perfect score would be 115 points. If you scored in the 50-60 range you probably have an adequate collection of coping strategies for most common sources of stress. However, you should keep in mind that the higher your score, the greater your ability to cope with stress in an effective and healthful manner.⌉ *SEE Liz*

Perhaps you are unpleasantly surprised at how many areas of your life indicate the presence of stress and how inadequately you are coping. Remember that stress need not be triggered by one monumental event such as death or divorce. Stress can sneak up on us bits at a time or grow into a monster within, eating away at our mental, emotional and physical well-being.

⌈ Here are some of the effects of stress and how they show up in our bodies:

- Headaches
- Non-specific ailments ("I just don't feel good.")
- Muscle pains
- Breathing problems
- High blood pressure
- Diarrhea
- Sleep disruption
- Depression
- Frequent colds and flu
- Excess tension
- Feelings of hopelessness
- Quick temper
- Sexual dysfunction

Allison, Lynn (1993). Natural Stress - Busters ⌉

▼ ▼ ▼

And here are the negative ways many of us have learned to cope with stress in the past:

- Overeating
- Drinking alcohol
- Using drugs or smoking
- Taking medication such as tranquilizers and "uppers" and "downers"
- Becoming aggressive
- Withdrawing into our shells
- Avoiding social situations and becoming hermits
- Acting in compulsive ways: over-exercising, crying, becoming embroiled in a hobby or sport, watching too much television, etc.
- Losing concentration
- Worrying
- Reacting violently

Allison, Lynn (1993). Natural Stress-Busters

Many people begin to look at these negative patterns as normal.

You can become so accustomed to compulsive behavior, rudeness, and other kinds of negativity that you forget how nice—and possible—it is to be healthy!

You are not coping with stress by using any of the previously mentioned escape hatches. On the contrary, you are actually putting more stress into your life by avoiding the root cause of your anxiety and dealing with your symptoms in negative ways.

Dr. Richard F. Gerson, the director of the Men's Spa at The World of Palm-Aire in Pompano Beach, Florida, is a well-known expert and lecturer on stress management. He points out:

"While it's true that stress is caused, to a great extent, by our daily lives, the actual problem lies within you. You create your own stress level and you feel it inside, both in immediate and in long-term effects it can have on your health."

▼ ▼ ▼

Gerson recommends the D.R.E.A.M. approach to conquering stress, his formula of Diet, Relaxation, Exercise, Attitude, and Motivation. To his formula, I will add my own favorite stress-busters: compassion and humor.

You need to temper your stress-busting routine with compassion delegated to yourself and to others. By learning how to forgive yourself and tolerate what we once considered intolerable behavior to those around us, we automatically reduce stress.

By regarding unfunny instances with a modicum of humor, we are able to defuse what could be a stress-producing situation.

(Something to laugh about...)

YOU KNOW IT'S GOING TO BE A BAD DAY WHEN:

- You wake up face down on the pavement.
- You call Suicide Prevention and they put you on hold.
- You put your bra on backwards and it fits better.
- You see a 60 Minute TV news team waiting in your office.
- Your birthday cake collapses from the weight of the candles.
- You want to put on the clothes you wore home from last night's party and there aren't any.
- You turn on the news and they're showing emergency routes out of the city.
- Your twin forgets your birthday.
- You wake up to discover that your waterbed broke and then realize you don't have a waterbed!
- Your horn goes off accidentally and remains stuck as you follow a group of Hell's Angels on the freeway.
- Your spouse wakes up feeling amorous and *you* have a headache!

▼ ▼ ▼

▼   ▼   ▼

Chapter Two

STRESS AND

GENDER

Both men and women suffer from stress, but I believe in today's society, women are under particular duress. Research shows that American women today work an average of 287 more hours per year than they did in 1969, adding nearly seven weeks work time annually to our already over-burdened load.

We have been catapulted into dual careers as working women and homemakers. For the first time in history, we are expected to be breadwinners as well as bread bakers.

It's no wonder women are experiencing a host of stress-related symptoms, including a most alarming rise in eating disorders.

"Women feel so out of control with their lives, they desperately try to control their bodies," explains Adrienne Ressler, a staff psychologist at the Renfrew Center, a residential care facility in Philadelphia and Coral Springs, Florida.

▼ ▼ ▼

"They feel torn and pulled in a dozen different directions and use food as the escape hatch."

Film maker Katherine Gilday, in her moving documentary *The Famine Within*, chronicles the pressures women face in today's body-conscious world and how a growing number of them are either starving or eating themselves to death- trying to fill the emotional famine within.

Overeating is merely one way we cope with unhealthy stress. Some of us turn to drugs, smoking, medication, exercise, withdrawal and other forms of retreat to temporarily deal with the painful and often debilitating symptoms of stress.

The media isn't helping. There are so many dual and contradictory messages out there, it's a wonder we're sane at all!

We are told by women's magazines how to cook healthful meals in 30 minutes flat. And then we're told by gourmet magazines that nothing short of four-star cuisine, starting from scratch using exotic ingredients, qualifies for culinary success.

▼ ▼ ▼

We're told to give our children "quality" time, but who's there to deal with the flooding washing machine during the allotted "quality" time?

We're encouraged to have careers and have children. Doesn't anybody realize that both are essentially full-time jobs? Most of the working mothers I know are extremely upset leaving their babies in day-care centers so they can work to provide a second income.

Despite the fact that many so-called experts say we can "have it all," the reality of today's world finds many of us tumbling into a sinking sense of nothingness. We are trying to do too much in too little time.

I vividly remember the nightmares of coping with a sick child and being forced into work, or having to work overtime knowing the day-care center would have my scalp by the time I picked up my year-old daughter. Talk about stress! I recall careening around the corner one day, en route to the day-care center and smashing into a parked car in my haste! It was my first and only accident, thank goodness, but this taught me a valuable lesson in stress-management: don't take your anxiety on the road!

A great many working moms with four or five children and no husband are forced into taking tedious, dead-end jobs to put food on the table.

These women are fighting for their lives and need down-to-earth, practical advice on how to maintain their sanity rather than lectures on scheduling "quality time."

Don't Fall for Media Hype

It's not easy being a woman today so don't ever think of yourself as a failure if you don't meet the plastic, societal standards set in magazines.

The mixed messages we get from the media tell us one thing, while the reality of our daily lives is another matter.

▼ ▼ ▼

Very few working women I know manage to successfully juggle their kids, homemaking, jobs, exercise routine and kitchen duties without lots of supportive help.

We are caught in a fast-forward society that doesn't leave enough room for running in slow motion. Machines cannot operate in fast forward without eventually burning out. How can we expect more from our human selves? We must learn to practice what Dr. Hans Selye called "altruistic egotism"—looking out for oneself while still servicing others.

This is not a fancy term for selfishness. This is a credo for sanity. Take care of yourself and you'll be more loving and helpful toward your loved ones.

Selye emphasizes the need to be honest with yourself and set personal limits.

"Are you a turtle or a race horse?" he asked. "Set your life's structure around your personality and your goals, not those of anyone else."

Forget what your mother wants you to be, or your husband expects of you. Stop being a martyr to your children and the ever-patient sounding board for your friends. Start setting necessary limits in your life to reduce stress and preserve your sense of balance.

"Something has got to give," a high-powered friend of mine confided after one of our daily workouts. "I can't keep running from home to work to the gym to the day-care center and still have my sanity."

This woman is frustrated because she is trying to be too many things to too many people. She is absolutely right when she cries out, "Something has got to give." Don't let it be your health and welfare! Let others learn how to give to *you*.

▼ ▼ ▼

Dr. Joyce Brothers, in her excellent book, *The Successful Woman* (Simon and Schuster), quotes 1986 Nobel Prize winner Dr. Rota Levi-Montalcini:

"It is very dangerous for people to live in a state of obsession, always worrying about careers or success. It is egocentric. We must keep our minds open to the problems of a larger society."

Dr. Brothers adds that there are basically two categories of working mothers: those who enjoy the challenge of juggling home life and career and those who would genuinely prefer to stay home with their children and forget about pursuing career goals.

Many of these women have dropped out of the work force, says Brothers, citing "burnout" and stress as the reasons. However, she believes that the true underlying cause is one of priorities.

"These women have subconsciously reordered their priorities," she writes. "They no longer crave success. It is as simple as that. However, when they leave their jobs, they cite burnout as the reason because they truly believe they have been stressed to the point of ineffectiveness. Burned out."

Dr. Estelle Ramey, of Georgetown University Medical School, explains that these women have really just lost "the motive force."

When you are filled with motivation to do a task, you sail through your duties with seemingly inexhaustible energy. However, when you lose that drive, that loving feeling, your job at hand becomes drudgery.

"The women who give up their careers are doing the right thing for the wrong reason," says Brothers. "They are really listening to their inner selves and choosing the way of life they really want."

▼ ▼ ▼

There is nothing to feel guilty about if you look into the mirror and say, "I've had enough! I'm getting off this boat before it sinks."

However, as Dr. Judith Crist, the director of Crist Counseling Center of Boca Raton, Florida, points out:

"Not every woman can afford to leave her job. There are many women who are the sole supporters of their households and must work. They do not have the choice that Dr. Brothers talks about."

For these women, a change of attitude and strategy can be the answer. Reach out, get help, cut corners whenever and wherever you can.

"I advise women to plan time for themselves," says Dr. Crist. "You must try to strike a balance in your life. You cannot keep giving to others if you don't set aside time for yourself. You can't be a wife, mother, worker, and household quarterback 24 hours a day."

Crist, a busy psychotherapist, has developed her own strategy to cope with her stressful career.

"I see clients Monday through Thursday," she says. "On Fridays, I pack up my briefcase, Dictaphone and notes along with my beach chair and head for the beach. There, under the shade of a palm tree, I go over my material and dictate my letters. I also carry along my portable phone so that I can touch base with the office in case of emergencies.

"For four hours I feel as if I'm in a tropical paradise and can come back to my work feeling rejuvenated and refreshed."

Work out a plan that is best suited to your lifestyle. Some of us need daily respite from our chores to recharge our batteries. One high-powered executive I know takes a walk whenever she feels the onset of stress.

She simply walks around her office building for as long as it takes to regain her sense of composure and balance.

Others may feel that a couple of hours during the weekend spent shopping, walking or going to a movie is enough.

▼ ▼ ▼

Personally, I need at least an hour of exercise each day to balance my life as a writer. After sitting at my computer for hours on end, I need to stretch my muscles, my mind and my eyes by focusing on the outside world.

Cutting back on responsibility, even for a short period of time, can also help restore balance during a stressful period of your life.

I was juggling several jobs a few years ago, and the extra duty mixed with domestic chores was throwing me into a frantic tizzy.

A very dear friend offered to take the children for a week, at her home. Although she had four kids of her own, she volunteered to alleviate the burden for me. I had a week of unbelievable peace and rest. I came home from work, took a long solitary walk and enjoyed a quiet dinner without the clutter and clamor of children. My girls, in turn, enjoyed their adventure and learned what it's like to be part of a large family. In turn, I baby-sat for my friend's brood to allow her and her husband a few Saturday nights on the town.

"There are times," says Dr. Crist, "when we get overloaded with stressful events. I call it 'pileup.' If you have several distressful things happen in your life—like the loss of a loved one, losing a job or illness, you are allowed to feel stressed out. You are allowed to step back and call time out. It's okay to feel down when you simply cannot cope with too much outside interference."

I know a busy restaurateur who thoroughly enjoys her job, but keeps Sundays and Mondays for herself.

"I close up the restaurant and spend quality time with my family and my hobbies," she says. "I don't schedule any social events and my friends understand that I need to be away from people for a while. When you are constantly interacting with others, it's essential to pull back and regroup."

There is a time to set limits, to take time out for yourself without feeling guilty. Children can help with age-appropriate chores. Husbands can shoulder their share of household re-

▼ ▼ ▼

sponsibility. You'll be surprised how capable your family can be once you put your foot down and change dependent behavior.

I'll never forget the Christmas Eve dinner I spent at the home of my dear friend, Lillian Wolfe, many years ago. Lillian was a divorced mother of two boys, aged ten and twelve. She gathered together a bunch of us single women for a contribution to the lonely heart's club!

Even though Lillian is Jewish, she celebrated all holidays because of the love and camaraderie she embraced as a person. I was feeling rather depressed when I arrived at her spotless duplex. It was the first time I had been away from my own children at Christmas as they were spending this holiday with their father.

Lillian's sons greeted me at the door with gifts they'd purchased from their allowances. They offered the other women and me cocktails and proceeded to serve a delicious meal.

The boys served the dinner and cleared the table with all the aplomb of professional waiters. In the meantime, they ate their dinner in the kitchen with several other kids who'd been invited for the evening.

When the meal was done, Lillian's handsome sons cheerfully washed all the dishes. I sneaked a peak at them happily washing and drying dozens of plates and utensils, and I was awestruck when they began polishing the counters and wiping down the floor. They didn't grumble. They didn't whine or bicker. They were actually enjoying themselves!

I asked Lillian, who worked as a publicist, what her secret was—were the boys always this supportive? Or was this just a special occasion?

"Of course not," she replied. "The boys have chores and do all the housework. They take turns cooking with recipes and lists I provide. This is their house, too, and I expect them to carry their load."

Let's not forget that in days gone by, children did have chores to perform and did them gladly. I think that in today's

▼ ▼ ▼

society, we've been brainwashed into coddling our kids against the reality of life. That's why we have so many frustrated and insecure young adults. They have been raised—by us—to believe that everything comes to those who wait for Mommy to bring it to them. Life's not like that. You have to get what you want the old-fashioned way: by earning it.

STRESS AND UNHEALTHY GUILT

One of the best and most readable experts on guilt and its consequences is Dr. Joan Borysenko, who wrote *Minding the Body, Mending the Mind* (Bantam) and my favorite book, *Guilt is the Teacher, Love is the Lesson* (Warner Books).

Dr. Borysenko, along with her charming husband, Myrin, have devoted their lives and careers to helping others achieve spiritual and emotional peace within themselves.

The attractive therapist almost drove herself to the grave with an unwieldy work schedule. She learned to slow down, like most of us eventually do, the hard way.

"I suffered for many years with unhealthy guilt," she says. "My lack of self-awareness had crippled me with illness, poor relationships, anxiety, depression, panic and perfectionism. Finally, I was forced to surrender and face the inner pain of shame. It is still easier for me, at times, to lose myself in work and pretend everything is fine instead of facing the consequences. But I have learned that self-deceit can be disastrous. Escaping the moment may make the present more comfortable, but it makes the future more difficult."

Borysenko outlines twenty-one signs of unhealthy guilt in *Guilt is the Teacher, Love is the Lesson*. Here are some of the signs that may be tearing you apart. Read through the list and see how many of these expressions apply to you:

1. I'M OVERCOMMITTED.

Taking on too many projects and responsibilities is the sign of unhealthy guilt. This habit is a major cause of stress

▼ ▼ ▼

and is fed by our inability to say "no" both to our own needs and to the expectations of others. Overcommitment is one way we hope to recapture our feeling of love and self worth. But it is also an addiction that prevents us from facing the reality of emptiness within.

2. I REALLY KNOW HOW TO WORRY.

Boy! That's a wonderful one for most women I know. We have a terrible habit of worrying ourselves sick about things over which we have no control. If your daughter is late, all the worrying in the world won't bring her home on time. If bills must be paid, then either pay them and get it over with or stop worrying and get on with your life.

An expert I once interviewed suggested that compulsive worriers set aside a half hour each day and get all their worrying done with in one fell swoop! Set aside a corner of a room, sit in your "worry chair," set the alarm clock and worry yourself silly for one solid half-hour. Then turn off the switch and go about your business.

3. I'M A COMPULSIVE HELPER.

My dear neighbor is a shining example of an Earth Mother. She's a nurse, a mom, a wonderful wife to her rather slothful husband and seems happiest when catering, nurturing and otherwise busying herself with the needs of others. Unfortunately, she has created a network of hangers-on, including her own family, who have become totally dependent people. Borysenko says those who constantly give to others are really in dire need of love themselves.

"The process is like the blind leading the blind," she notes. "Both are likely to fall in a ditch."

▼ ▼ ▼

4. I'M ALWAYS APOLOGIZING FOR MYSELF.

Author Charlotte Davis Kasl, author of *Women, Sex, and Addiction* (Harper & Row), says women in particular are prone to belittling themselves.

"As one woman in group therapy told me, 'I say I'm wrong for breathing air. I need to say I'm right for a change.'"

Another elderly woman I know explained it's just easier to apologize and say you're wrong.

"Why make waves?" she says.

It's time we stop making lame excuses for everything that goes wrong in our lives—and the lives of others. It's time we stop blaming ourselves for inconsequential things like dinner being late or the house not being clean enough. Who cares? Who is measuring? It's time we stop setting ourselves up before an imaginary judge and jury, and start giving ourselves a sense of value and self-worth.

5. I OFTEN WAKE UP FEELING ANXIOUS OR HAVE PERIODS WHEN I AM ANXIOUS FOR DAYS AND WEEKS.

One of the major causes of stress is unnecessary anxiety over things and circumstances over which we really have no control. It's a horrible feeling, waking up in the middle of the night, with that achy and anxious feeling prompted by the "what ifs" and "should haves" of our days.

This anxious feeling is often a reflection of our own inner anger. When we learn how to deal with situations honestly and openly, and stop agonizing over what we can and cannot control, the anxiety goes away.

6. I'M ALWAYS BLAMING MYSELF.

As women, we tend to carry the burden of guilt and blame for whatever happens in our family. If our child fails an exam, it's our fault for not being a better parent. If we lose our jobs, we tend to personalize the action instead of realizing that cutbacks are inevitable in bad economic times. Pessimistic

▼ ▼ ▼

thinking is one of the most common signs of unhealthy guilt that leads to undue stress.

7. I WORRY WHAT OTHER PEOPLE THINK OF ME.

We spend an inordinate amount of time worrying what other people think about how we look, what we say and even what we think. Once you get in touch with your true feelings and develop a sense of self-confidence, you begin to stop attaching your sense of worth with the reaction of others.

As a wise Buddhist asked me when I told her I was tired of a certain family member treating me like a piece of dirt:

"Well, are you a piece of dirt?"

I replied, "Heck, no!" And that was the end of that. That simple question triggered a change in my reaction to that person's criticism and surprisingly, once I stopped overreacting, the barbs stopped.

8. I HATE IT WHEN PEOPLE ARE ANGRY AT ME.

As Dr. Borysenko points out, we're always sniffing the air for signs of anger in others. If the boss is quiet, we think he or she is ignoring us or is angry at something we've done.

We forget to call someone back and then procrastinate because we think she will be angry. When a person yells at us we shrink and withdraw instead of taking control of the situation and either confronting or diffusing the wrath. Your self worth is not dependent on whether someone likes you or not.

9. I'M NOT AS GOOD AS PEOPLE THINK I AM.

Many of us suffer from the "good little boy" or "good little girl" syndrome. We live our lives constantly trying to produce, be the perfect person and generally act out a generous, caring facade even when we feel like saying, "No!" This causes a lot of internal conflict. Take off the Superwoman cape and just be yourself.

Stop measuring yourself up to what you think are the standards of others. If you have always been Miss Perfect, you

▼ ▼ ▼

may be surprised to learn that your family and friends would enjoy seeing a different, more human side of your behavior.

10. I'M A DOORMAT.

The famous martyr complex almost always leads to anger when we try to stop playing victim. If you think you are getting Brownie points by doing twice as much as anybody else around the house and at the office, you are wrong.

Very few people like to be shown up or put under pressure by a "goody-two-shoes" who is always sighing and complaining about his or her work load. In effect, you are forcing others to assume the role of bad guy when you adopt the victim or doormat stance.

11. I NEVER HAVE TIME FOR MYSELF.

Well, make time. You know that exercise, meditation, rest and simply being alone for a while are good and healthy things you should do for yourself. Forget the excuses: the dishwasher needs unloading, the rug needs vacuuming, etc. These chores can and will wait. They can also be done by others. When we don't take time to enjoy life, then we are not really living. We're just playing another role.

12. I WORRY ABOUT BEING SELFISH.

Yes, I can just see the women out there nodding in recognition. We have long been conditioned to be selfless, not selfish in our lives.

If we allow ourselves to become stressed out and weak by giving, giving and still giving to others, we are draining our own batteries and won't be able to help others in the long run.

It is not being selfish when you tell your child that you do not want to play ball or buy him a candy bar when you're tired or broke. You are teaching a lesson in restraint and respect.

It is not selfish to tell your married daughter that you don't want to baby-sit every Saturday because you and your husband may want some free weekend time. It is not selfish to refuse to open your wallet every time a family member re-

▼ ▼ ▼

quests funds. Nor is it selfish to request that your mate learn to help you in the home. It's survival.

13. I CAN'T STAND CRITICISM.

This sign struck uncomfortably close to my home plate! I used to be terrible about criticism, unable to stand a single critical word or gesture. I'd agonize for days if someone took offense to my writing or found errors in my copy. I'm still not terrific about being on the receiving end of harsh words, but the following advice from a Buddhist teacher helped me look at criticism on another plane:

"If someone criticizes you and is right, that person is then a friend because he has done you a favor. You thank him for pointing out your error and learn from that mistake.

"However, if you are right and that person has wrongly accused or criticized you, why should you care about the words?"

14. I CAN'T SAY NO.

This little word provokes more guilt than any other I know. We are afraid someone might think we are bad or selfish if we refuse a request. We all can recall painful events in our lives when, if we had been forthright and honest, the simple word "no" would have avoided a confrontation or argument.

Sometimes "no" can be tempered with an option if you want to soften the blow. For example, your sister-in-law decides she wants to visit with her noisy kids next week and you've got a major project to complete. You hate to refuse your own sister, but having her brood in your home will be extremely stressful at this time.

Offer her an alternative, perhaps a month from now, when your work is completed.

▼ ▼ ▼

It's no secret that premenstrual syndrome, commonly called PMS, is no laughing matter. Despite the many jibes and jokes about the emotional highs and lows suffered by women shortly before their menstrual cycle, PMS does affect about 75 percent of all females.

According to Dr. Miriam Stoppard, in the most helpful book, *Everywoman's Medical Handbook* (Ballantine Books), PMS produces depression, aches, pains and changes in mood.

"It seems that these symptoms are linked with the production of female hormones estrogen and progesterone," she explains. "These hormones are both crucial to our mood and level of activity. It is not surprising that an imbalance can give rise to an array of symptoms now regarded seriously by the medical profession."

Indeed, major crimes (murder, suicide) and minor crimes such as shoplifting are 30 times more prevalent among women suffering from PMS. Be aware of your monthly cycles and if you find that you do have mild to severe symptoms during the days before your period, take special care to avoid undue stress.

You may want to seek medical advice from your doctor if the symptoms are uncontrollable. He or she may prescribe a hormone treatment that should be taken about four days before the symptoms usually arise.

Many women find that by eating smaller amounts of food more often they are able to alleviate the strain of PMS. High-fiber foods, including lots of fresh vegetables and fruits, do help relieve the symptoms.

Drink lots of fresh water, take vitamin B supplements and try Evening Primrose oil tablets that are available at your health food market. Avoid eating salty foods which aggravate fluid retention, a common symptom of PMS.

If you get particularly teary-eyed and emotional, stay away from major confrontations or decisions. I chart my menstrual cycles and make sure that the week before I am due, I do not

▼ ▼ ▼

plan major activities that can trigger PMS symptoms. Put off chores and duties that deplete your needed energy.

Certain yoga exercises can help ease the pain and discomfort of PMS. The Cobra, for example, is an excellent choice. Lie on your stomach, hands placed under your shoulders.

Breathe in deeply and lift your upper body off the floor. Raise your head and chest as high as you can comfortably without using your arms, then push up with your hands to arch your back. Hold for 30 seconds and release, bringing your chin back to the floor. Repeat once more.

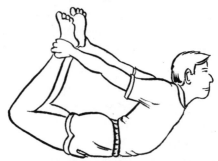

The Bow is another yoga pose that relieves the agony of female disorders as well as strengthening your back muscles. Lie on the floor, face down, and reach back to grab your ankles. Pull up on your ankles while raising your head and chest so that your body resembles a bow ready to spring its arrow. Gently rock back and forth to massage the pelvic area.

Another exercise taught to me by yoga expert Celeste Chiappetta, is wonderful any time of the month! Lie on your back, placing your buttocks as close as possible to a wall. Lift

▼ ▼ ▼

your legs against the wall for support and wiggle your bottom even closer, so that your body and legs form a 90-degree angle. Close your eyes and simply rest, allowing the blood to flow down through your legs. This is a super relaxation pose.

MEN AND STRESS

The demands of raising a family today are high, from the sheer economic burden of daily support to the stress of dealing with a difficult economic situation. Men today are faced with an uncertain future. Companies once thought of as bastions of security are laying off employees by the thousands. Smaller firms are downsizing in an effort to tighten their financial belts.

In addition to this squeeze play, men who are also the fathers of children face increased health-care and educational costs. Children stay at home longer. They seek higher and higher education often at great expense and burden to their families.

The media, once again, plays carelessly with the male role, offering images of stalwart, ever-patient dads who meet the economic demands of their families and are also great husbands. These successful, ever-willing fathers seldom lose their temper and never show emotional frustration. When is the last time you saw a television dad break down and cry on camera because he lost his job or can't pay the rent? Yet in many American homes, men are struggling just to keep their financial heads above water, let alone be the ideal pillars of family strength.

"I feel that I have to be a breadwinner, supportive parent and enthusiastic lover as well as understanding husband, gourmet barbecue chef and all-round good guy," laments one 50-year-old man I know. "I just want to take some of the pressure off."

It's no wonder that many middle-aged men are jumping ship, leaving their families high and dry.

▼ ▼ ▼

I'm certainly not condoning this irresponsible behavior. In fact, running away from home is merely a childish response to stress. It's always better to deal with situations before they reach the breaking point. Running away seldom solves anything, and the guilt you feel abandoning your family only compounds your stress.

Try to communicate your frustrations instead of burying them. Express your innermost fears instead of hiding them in your heart. You'll be surprised at how your spouse and family will respond to your honesty. Many couples tend to drift apart after years of marriage, each party thinking the other is either too busy or uninterested in their problems.

Maybe it is time to get back on track with your mate. Sit down like you used to, as newlyweds, and re-examine your mutual goals and dreams. I think most couples will admit that despite the hassles and arguments, they still deeply love and care for one another.

Men have a gender and cultural tendency to bury their innermost feelings, thinking it is unmanly to express weakness, frustration and fear. But it is only human to have and express these worries. And who better to share and understand them than your mate?

Women are not mind readers even though many men swear their wives are blessed with a sixth sense! If you, as a man, are troubled by office politics, financial woes or simply a fear of growing old, why not discuss your feelings with your mate? You'll be surprised how, once the air is cleared, she may take some of that stressful pressure off.

Let me give you an example.

A friend of mine constantly nagged her husband about every possible thing from money to his sloppiness. She'd rant and rave both in public and in private, scarcely giving the poor guy a moment's peace.

"You're just a lazy slob," she'd yell. "Joe next door makes twice the money you make and he's not even as educated as you are. And he takes Emily out dancing every Friday while

▼ ▼ ▼

you sit there in front of the boob tube and watch that damn ball game!"

We all felt very sorry for the husband who never responded to her tirades. He seemed to shrink into his shell and never said a word in retaliation.

The Secret Fear Within

Then one day, after a few too many uncharacteristic drinks at a social event, he broke down in uncontrollable tears and sobbed:

"I'm so sorry I've let you and the kids down. I know I'm a failure and I feel miserable about it. I can't stand my life anymore and I'm even beginning to think of suicide."

His wife stood there, transfixed. Her stoic, silent husband was shaking with heart-rending sobs. We could visibly see her face change from its hard, aggressive mask to a softer, more compassionate image.

As her face dissolved into love, she moved toward him and placed her arms around his shoulders, holding him closely.

"I never realized," she stammered. "I always thought you didn't care about us because you never talked about your feelings. I thought you had everything so under control you didn't need us."

Together, they became a team once more. The wife realized that her anger and chiding came from her own frustration. She was the one who felt left out and abandoned because of his lack of communication. The only way she knew how to get a rise out of her husband was to nag.

"That's how my parents lived their lives," she admitted. "Nagging was the only way I knew how to communicate."

It was quite amazing that once her husband opened up his heart and mind so that she could enter, the pair became inseparable. He learned to share his stress, and she felt truly needed and loved.

▼ ▼ ▼

Where there is love, there is also the capacity for understanding and forgiveness. Sometimes you have to trust and let go.

Another top executive I know began criticizing his wife for the smallest expenditures. She bought a car cover and he hit the roof. She had her first manicure in 30 years and he ranted and raved for days. This man was earning well over $100,000 a year and could afford dozens of car covers and manicures.

In the meantime, his saint of a wife continued to cook and clean for him and their three children, and did everything in her power to make their house a home.

Finally, their arguments came to a head and he admitted he was extremely frightened about his job, their future and his own mortality. They had three children to support and put through college, several mortgages to pay, and he was tired of the worry and aggravation of his domestic responsibilities. He expressed, for the very first time to his wife, that he was fed up with shouldering the massive financial burden and having grown-up kids still feeding off the fruits of his labor.

"I was out of the house at 16," he said. "I never dared ask my parents for a dime. First of all, they didn't have it and secondly, we were taught from childhood to make our own way in life. So what went wrong with my own kids? Why was I continuing to support fully grown adults? I've been earning a living since I was eight years old. When is it my turn to relax?"

He and his wife sat down and discussed what they were going to do with the rest of their lives and decided to start enjoying themselves today instead of always living and planning for the future. He put several of his properties up for sale, told the children that from now on they'd have to pay half their tuition and room and board, and took his wife on a long overdue cruise to nowhere.

"It was the first time in 25 years that we went away together—and not to visit family," she laughed. "It was like a second honeymoon."

▼ ▼ ▼

You don't owe your children—especially grown children—any more than you can afford both emotionally and financially to give.

My husband's father died when he was five years old. His mother, an uneducated, diminutive Italian immigrant, was left with 11 children to raise. She taught them at a very early age that whatever they wanted—a bike, hockey stick and most of all, a college education—could be theirs if they worked for it.

The children grew up to be very responsible and successful individuals despite their lack of material comforts. If they truly wanted to go to college, they worked for the money or obtained scholarships.

Comedian Jerry Lewis ended a recent Labor Day Telethon with a moving speech on how much his wife and kids meant to him. He said, in effect, that although he never graduated high school and was dirt poor for much of his youth, he always placed family love and values ahead of financial gain and popularity.

Now, in his golden years, Lewis still pays tribute to the love and support of his wife and family as his yardstick of success.

If you want to pursue money and power for your own sake, then by all means, go for it. But if something deep down doesn't feel right and you dread the thought of taking one more day on the corporate treadmill, sit back and re-evaluate the direction of your life.

Sometimes, the road less traveled is far more interesting and rewarding for everyone concerned.

▼ ▼ ▼

SEXUAL PERFORMANCE

Pop media touts the joy of sex while the reality of today's stressful environment has made sex a nightmare for many men. Instead of emphasizing the joy and love of sex, the media has placed the emphasis on sexual performance. Some experts believe this has led to an increase in sexual impotence in men.

The late Dr. Paavo Airola, in his fascinating book *Worldwide Secrets for Staying Young* (Health Plus), reveals that men in many so-called primitive cultures are able to enjoy sex well into their nineties and even beyond.

He credits such virility to a happy, positive attitude and healthy lifestyle that includes foods from nature's bounty and little red meat, alcohol or tobacco.

Dr. Airola, regarded as one of the leading researchers into longevity says:

"There are two sources of long life. One is a gift of nature, and it is the pure air and clear water of the mountain, the fruit of the earth, peace, rest, and the soft warm climate of the highlands.

"The second source is within us. He lives long who enjoys life and bears no jealousy of others, whose heart harbors no malice or anger, who sings a lot and cries a little, who rises and retires with the sun, who likes to work and knows how to rest."

Dr. Airola, after studying the sexual activity of many centenarians, concluded that we do not stop sexual activity because we grow old—we grow old because we stop sexual activity. Men who appreciate sex for its own sake can look forward not only to a long sex life but also to a longer and happier life itself!

Almost without exception, these oldsters revealed that their secret to a happy, fulfilled and sexually active life was learning to pace themselves, living moderately and modestly without abusing their bodies or minds with stressful factors.

▼ ▼ ▼

If sexual performance is giving you stress, relax and take the emphasis away from the end result and put more time, love and effort into the preliminaries. Most women I know vastly prefer the kissing, cuddling and hugging before intercourse than the actual act itself.

Sex is very important to our physical and mental well-being and is a wonderful stress-buster! Don't let performance stand in your way of enjoying one of nature's greatest gifts.

▼ ▼ ▼

Chapter Three

MIND OVER
MATTER

It's important to tackle and diffuse stress as soon as we feel the physical and psychological symptoms coming on. Stress is the underlying cause of a host of symptoms of all illnesses, and a great deal of our discomfort can be headed off at the pass—if we use our minds to identify and dissipate stressors.

If we look at the word "disease" and see it as meaning "dis-ease" of the mind and body, we realize that most of our bouts with illness occur during or immediately after a particularly stressful time in our lives.

It's no coincidence that we come down with the flu right after our mother-in-law arrives for an extended visit. It's not unusual for people to get digestive disorders when they're under pressure at home or on the job.

When we are off balance or not at ease with ourselves, we become prime targets for disease. Therefore, it is essential to learn how to recognize the *very first signs* of stress before it has a chance to kick our body out of balance.

▼ ▼ ▼

Buddhists, like many spiritual beings, are wonderful proponents of mind-body balance. They practice for years learning how to keep their minds centered and their bodies balanced accordingly.

Buddhism is actually more of a psychology than a religion. Like many Eastern philosophies, it expounds the belief that negative thoughts and emotions destroy the body. By controlling the mind through techniques of positive thinking and meditation, you can keep yourself healthy and stress-free.

The young American Buddhist Thubten Chodron was born in an upper middle-class Jewish home and gave up all her material goods to pursue a higher spiritual goal in life. Chodron shaved her head, spent years studying Buddhism in Tibet, and wrote a most informative and clear book on the Buddhist philosophy. It's called *Open Heart, Clear Mind* (Snow Lion Publications) and contains illuminating anecdotes on how meditation can help give your life new meaning and clarity.

Meditation is not an exotic, out-of-this-world technique that "weird" people practice. It is a most helpful tool to give your mind a much needed vacation from the stress and pressures of daily life.

Meditation works like a spiritual vacuum, cleaning house in our minds. We learn how to remove deadly negativity and allow peaceful, calm, loving positive thoughts to enter. Anger, jealousy and hate are examples of negative emotions that cause stress. Love, compassion and peacefulness are positive emotions that bring us joy and happiness.

My dear friend, the Reverend Bob Harrington, popularly known as the "Chaplain of Bourbon Street," says most of us suffer from "spiritual cholesterol."

"We spend so much time clogging our mental and emotional arteries with negative thinking, there's no room for the good stuff to flow," he says.

▼ ▼ ▼

48

LET GO OF EMOTIONAL GARBAGE AND LET THE GOOD FEELINGS FLOW

Buddhism also teaches the value of non-attachment. When we get "hung up" with caring for all our worldly goods—TV, VCR, computer, house, car, boat, etc.—our focus is narrowed to things that could easily be destroyed by acts of God or nature. Even our loved ones can leave us through death or desertion.

Therefore, we are asking to be disappointed when we pin all of our hopes and channel all of our energies on the pursuit of "things." Think about *your* stress. Isn't most of it rooted in acquiring money, keeping your possessions intact and trying to juggle a dozen duties simultaneously? Wouldn't it be wonderful to be able to enjoy the moment instead of agonizing about yesterday and worrying about tomorrow?

You can train your mind to develop healthier habits. Meditation and making a conscious effort to live each day…each hour…each moment in a positive light is the route leading to a stress-free existence.

Let's look at what Chodron calls the "Cracker Theory":

You are holding a cracker. You can feel, smell, taste and otherwise see that what you have in your hands is indeed a cracker.

Now crush that cracker to crumbs. What do you have now? Are the crumbs that fill your palm and spill onto the floor the same cracker you held moments before? All you have now is a zillion particles of what once was a whole cracker.

Where or what is the real cracker? Is it the object you once held or is it the sum of the zillion particles. According to the Buddhists, neither is the real cracker because the word "cracker" is simply a label we've attached to an object. A cracker, like a feeling or emotion, is not permanent and does not exist by itself. We give thoughts and objects life and meaning. We attach importance to situations or relationships.

▼ ▼ ▼

How often have you fretted about a meeting or appointment, worrying about who is going to say what or how well you will perform? How often have you driven yourself crazy over that registered-letter notice? What if it's from the IRS? What if I did something terribly wrong?

Nine times out of ten, our fears are grossly unfounded and we breathe great sighs of relief, vowing never again to allow ourselves to endure such stress for nothing. Until the next time...

By learning how to control our minds and stop wasting energy over non-issues, we save our minds for positive actions. We think more clearly. We produce more efficiently.

Let's look at another example. Most people would call the Grand Canyon one of the world's greatest wonders. Most of us would use the words "magnificent" and "beautiful" to describe this awesome geographic structure.

And yet, conceivably, an environmentalist could look at the Grand Canyon as a horrible example of ecological erosion. To this person, the Grand Canyon is ugly—not beautiful or magnificent. All objects, thought or emotions are merely a matter of your own perspective.

What is real and important to one person may be meaningless to another...What is beautiful to one pair of eyes can be hideous to someone else's...What food tastes good to you or I may seem awful to someone from another culture.

We create our own stress by getting carried away with so-called important events in our lives. By learning to skew our thinking, we can shrink the importance and effect these stressful objects have and actually befriend them. For example, instead of worrying about an upcoming competition, consider it a welcome challenge. Instead of focusing on winning, remind yourself that you're going to have a wonderful time competing.

By learning how to become mentally and emotionally "detached" from the stressors of life, we are better able to

▼ ▼ ▼

maintain a calm and content demeanor. We are also better able to deal with situations in an effective manner.

Consider these wise words from the Buddha:

"If you desire every joy,
Completely forsake all attachment.
By forsaking all attachment
A most excellent ecstasy is found.

So long as you follow attachment
Satisfaction is never found.
Whoever reverses attachment
With wisdom attains satisfaction."

Buddhism is not the only philosophy to embrace the idea of letting go and allowing nature to take its course. My favorite passage from the Bible is also a glowing testament to the importance of "going with the flow."

"For everything its season and every activity under heaven its time:
a time to be born and a time to die;
a time to plant and a time to uproot;
a time to kill and a time to heal;
a time to pull down and a time to build up;
a time to weep and a time to laugh;
a time for mourning and a time for dancing;
a time to scatter stones and a time to gather them;
a time to embrace and a time to refrain from embracing;
a time to seek and a time to lose;
a time to keep and a time to throw away;
a time to tear and a time to mend;
a time for silence and a time for speech;
a time to love and a time to hate;
a time for war and a time for peace..."

—Ecclesiastes 3, The New English Bible

▼ ▼ ▼

We cannot force or push the natural order of things. To do so is not only foolish, but also stressful.

Proverbs 27 advises us:

"Do not flatter yourself about tomorrow,
for you never know what a day will bring forth."

We can dramatically reduce the stress in our lives by thinking less about our material and emotional worlds and making peace with the forces that flow through our lives.

Open your mind to the reality that there is a universal flow and force to life that you cannot control. You can spend a fortune building the most luxurious home in the world. You can agonize for months over its construction, decor and furnishings. You can pin all your pride and dreams on this beautiful home that will make you the happiest, most revered person on the block.

And then a devastating hurricane strikes with winds gusting to 168 miles an hour. Your beautiful home is shattered and your dreams are reduced to rubble.

Everything you thought was so important is gone. But what is really important, what you have left, is your life and those loved ones around you.

Remember that each and every one of us wants one thing out of life and that's happiness. To achieve happiness we must look for it whenever and wherever we can. Let's train our minds to look for the good around us instead of the bad; the beauty instead of the beast. Let's learn to accept life at face value, without grandiose expectations or egotistical dreams.

HOW TO TRAIN YOUR MIND TO BE STRESS-FREE

Because we are human beings and not machines that can be reprogrammed with the touch of a button, it's not easy turning our thinking around. Even highly spiritual people can "lose it" every now and then.

But persistent training on a daily basis can help you build

▼ ▼ ▼

"mind muscles" that are strong and positive. Roy Eugene Davis, the founder and leader of the Center for Spiritual Awareness in Rabun, Georgia, recommends the following routine for building a better mind and spirit:

1. DAILY MEDITATION

Meditate on a regular, daily schedule for the relaxation benefits. Dr. Davis recommends at least one hour, but many people obtain benefits from 20-minute sessions. Schedule a specific interlude each day when you can be quiet, without interruptions, and enjoy your solitude.

You can use a meditation tape, such as the ones sold in many metaphysical stores or through the mail, or you can tape one of the meditations at the end of this chapter. Or, if you are lucky enough to have access to a meditation group headed by a qualified leader, you can learn to develop your own method of meditation.

▼ ▼ ▼

2. AVOID ENVIRONMENTAL STRESS

Unless you are an extremely strong-minded or highly trained meditator, it's pretty hard to keep your stress level under control when the phone's ringing, the baby's crying and the television is on full blast.

Even if you handle challenges well, external pressures can cause internal stress buildup. Keep your home environment as peaceful and as nurturing as possible. It may sound simplistic and old-fashioned, but living in a cluttered or dirty environment can create stress. Keep your home clean and well-ordered. Make the lighting soft and soothing instead of glaring. Avoid loud, raucous music and television shows and choose softer themes instead (If you've got teenagers, buy headsets for their stereo!).

Decorate your home in relaxing colors: blues, greens and pastels. Display treasured items and photographs that you can look to for warmth and comfort on "down" days. Keep a book or booklet of positive affirmations or sayings by your bedside to soothe and calm your spirit at night.

Grow plants or flowers—even if you live in a high-rise. Herb gardens can be relaxing both to the mind and to the senses. Mint, for example is easily grown in window pots and adds an aura of peace to your environment.

Avoid reading or watching upsetting news stories. There's an epidemic of tabloid-style format in both print and television news coverage. I'm not saying you should avoid reading or learning about what is going on in the world, but try to balance the gloom-and-doom stories with more uplifting fare. Read the comics before reading the front page headlines! And instead of watching the more violent and racy programs on television, tape old movies to view in the evening.

If there is an unresolved, job-related dilemma, remember that it will have to wait until the morning. You can better cope with your problems with a fresh and rested mind.

▼ ▼ ▼

Schedule restful vacations periodically. These needn't be expensive ventures. My husband and I often pack up and escape to a nearby inexpensive inn just for Saturday night.

The three-hour drive is just a vacation in itself. We play our favorite music en route, enjoy a relaxing dinner away from telephones and the noise of our busy suburb and return Sunday afternoon joyfully refreshed.

If you can't get away for a night, walk to the nearest park. Bring a good book or simply allow time to enjoy the foliage and peace of the greenery around you. Schedule *at least* three hours each week to get away from responsibilities and recharge your batteries.

3. EXERCISE AND REST

Maintain a regular exercise routine. For some of us, this may be a daily exercise class, for others a daily brisk walk. Simple acts of gardening, hauling wood or even cleaning your house can provide a needed respite from all the mental work done in this society.

Our entire generation has wandered so far from the physical side of nature that stress is running rampant. Exercise is one way of diffusing excess energy and balancing the mind-body budget.

Yoga is especially helpful in alleviating stress and re-establishing harmony in your body's energy flow. There are many kinds of yoga, ranging from relaxation and breathing techniques to very physical hatha yoga. The best way to find a suitable class is through trial and error. Very often, finding just the right teacher helps you stick with a yoga class.

Unfortunately, in my experience, too many yoga teachers are aloof and demanding. However, there are thousands who are sympathetic and very well informed. It's worth the small effort to find the right one for you.

While yoga is especially good for stress-busting, any form of regular exercise is beneficial. If you don't have access to an exercise studio or YMCA, check the many valuable video

▼   ▼   ▼

tapes available. Or look to your television listings for programs geared to easy exercise.

Our chapter on Exercise and Stress outlines simple but effective exercises to help reduce stress.

Get plenty of rest. That old adage, "Early to bed, early to rise" is still very much a truism. Use the early morning hours to exercise, meditate or read inspirational passages. You'll find yourself much better able to cope with daily pressures if you've set aside a peaceful time of solitude for yourself. Sleep as many hours as needed to rest your body—no more, no less. Each one of us has a personal time clock. Some need only a few hours to feel rested while others need far more.

4. DIET AND NUTRITION

Choose a natural, simple food plan. Many stress experts say a vegetarian diet is best to combat stress. Pastas, grains and fresh fruits and vegetables have a calming affect on your system and do not aggravate the digestive tract.

Find out which foods are best for your personal needs and lifestyle. Avoid fatty and overprocessed foods such as candy, commercially baked goods and refined sugar. If you eat meat, choose lean cuts and consume no more than four ounces daily.

Eat when you are hungry and don't overload the system in the evening hours. This practice not only disrupts your sleep, but also packs on extra weight! We'll talk more about controlling stress through nutrition and developing a lifetime diet plan later in this book.

5. REMAIN FOCUSED ON YOUR PURPOSE

Take a few minutes and write down the goals in your life. What do you want to accomplish and how do you plan to achieve your goals? You may have never really thought about this question before, but it is ultimately a most important one. If you want to become rich and famous, outline short- and long-range plans on how you intend to achieve your goals.

▼ ▼ ▼

If you plan to create a self-sufficient lifestyle for you and your family, then it certainly helps to see your goals and plans on paper. Take time to write down these essential items. Following a black-and-white script for success helps you remain focused on your goals and makes it less likely to be led astray.

Now that you have a clearer picture in which direction you're headed, make a firm commitment to yourself to include behaviors and relationships that bolster your journey. Eliminate those behaviors and relationships that do not.

This may seem like a rather harsh measure, but in order to allow ourselves to grow and become the fully developed, stress-free and happy people we want to be, we must dump the garbage that's holding us back.

Many of you may be thinking, "But my family—my lazy daughter, possessive mother or jealous sibling—is the source of much of my stress and conflict. How can I let a family member go and eliminate that relationship?"

I don't think there are any clear-cut answers to this legitimate question, but many of us have come to terms with this issue by either taking control of disruptive relationships or setting limits on the amount of time we spend in them.

In many cases, taking positive action has actually helped improve negative relationships.

If money problems are hampering your lifestyle, open your mind and heart to the abundance around you. If you study the history of a number of individual success stories, you'll find the common thread. Great achievement always comes from maintaining a positive and clearly focused mental attitude.

Remember the nursery story about the little engine that kept saying, "I think I can, I think I can" and eventually accomplished a most incredible feat? Be that little engine. Don't let a pessimistic, defeatist attitude spoil your chance to live a fulfilled life. If you think you can, you will!

▼ ▼ ▼

6. BE SERVICE ORIENTED

Achieving your goals—financial or otherwise—and serving the community are not mutually exclusive. Again, when you examine the lives of the most successful men and women in our country you'll discover these people invariably give back to society a portion of what they receive.

Richard Simmons, the Clown Prince of Fitness, readily admits it is his genuine love of service that keeps him away from the candy bowl. Richard says it is his need to help others that keeps his own weight in check.

"Think always in terms of service," says Roy Eugene Davis. "Nature provides you with everything you need for comfortable, successful living. Once you learn to be open to the goodness of the universe, all you have to do is be dedicated to serving the cause of evolution."

For those of you who question this philosophy, let's look at a growing North American phenomenon. Mental health experts are beginning to see that stress is often triggered by what they call "emotional isolation."

"We don't know all the reasons why people are feeling alienated," says Michael Lewis, a developmental scientist at the University of Medicine and Dentistry at New Jersey and the author of *Shame: The Exposed Self* (The Free Press, 1992). Between the economic crunch and the severe time restraints we are under, more Americans are retreating into lonely shells and focusing on themselves and their problems.

"When you focus on only yourself," says Lewis, "you sacrifice emotional ties to others and the sense of community that is essential to coping well with all sources of stress. There's so little in our society that is bringing us together. Politics are divisive and people are always on the move."

By giving of yourself—either financially or as a volunteer, or both—to your community, you can help regenerate healthy ties with others. By taking the focus off *your* problems and concentrating on greater issues and "the bigger picture,"

▼ ▼ ▼

you automatically diffuse your level of stress by putting your problems into perspective.

7. LET LOVE BE YOUR GUIDE

We all know people who operate solely from a negative position. They are rude, spiteful and walk around with giant chips on their shoulders. These folks are never happy and don't seem to be enjoying life no matter how materially successful they become. They have no love light in their lives. They live in a mean-spirited, selfish cocoon devoid of love and tenderness. Ultimately, they have no love because they don't love themselves.

If you respect yourself and in turn, love yourself, you will find love in others. When you love yourself, you will be good to yourself. You will contribute to your own welfare and spiritual growth. You will find time to rest and nurture yourself both in body and soul. Look for the good in life and in those around you, and you will begin to find nuggets of love everywhere you go.

Remember that your time on this earth is limited and that this is not a rehearsal. Even those who believe in reincarnation understand that how you live your life today determines the spiritual level of your return.

And if you believe that we only go around once, then why not have a good time!

MEDITATION EXERCISES

The Mutual of Omaha Insurance Company is now reimbursing patients for a program shown to reverse heart disease without drugs or surgery. The program includes a low-fat diet, exercise and meditation.

Meditation, even for a beginner, is the greatest tool you have to combat stress. It's like taking a mini-vacation for the mind anytime you need a break. You can meditate on the job, in your car when you are stopped at a red light, or anytime you need to escape the onslaught of stressors.

▼ ▼ ▼

Take at least 20 minutes a day to practice the following meditation and relaxation exercises. Tape the meditations on your cassette recorder if you are more comfortable with listening to the words instead of reading them. (Or, you may order these meditations already pre-recorded on a cassette tape, with soothing sounds of nature in the background, from Cool Hand Communications. The order form is located at the back of this book.)

Use proper form when you meditate. Sit tall and straight, cross legged on the floor if you can, and concentrate on keeping your spine in a vertical line and your shoulders down and relaxed. You may close your eyes or keep them slightly open to allow a small sliver of light to enter. This will help you avoid falling asleep. The goal of meditation is not to induce sleep but to relax and refresh the mind.

We meditate to clear the mind for the tasks at hand. If we meditate in the morning, we face the day with a calm and focused attitude. Because we are centered and stress-free, we are more energetic and productive in our work.

If we meditate in the evening, we fall asleep with the serenity of a small child unburdened by adult troubles and free of disruptive thoughts.

Don't be hard on yourself if your mind wanders during meditation. This is perfectly normal. Identify the disruption and let it go. Bring your focus back to the meditation as you would bring a small child who has drifted away back to the task at hand.

After a while, meditation becomes easier and more rewarding. Practice may never make perfect, but the rewards are enormous at any level.

1. MORNING MEDITATION

Before the family awakens and the hustle and bustle of the morning begins, take a few minutes to prepare your mind for the day to come. It really pays to give yourself that head start.

▼ ▼ ▼

Sit tall and straight, your spine supported and your shoulders relaxed. Let your arms fall comfortably by your side. Cross your knees in front of you or place your feet on the floor if you're sitting and let your hands rest, palms up, on your knees.

Close your eyes, letting a bit of light enter to keep you awake and alert.

Focus your attention on your breath. See your nostril, the tip of your nose, expand and contract as you inhale and exhale. Focus on your breathing, allowing all your cares and worries to dissolve with each "out" breath while you inhale peace and energy... Out with your stress, in with renewed energy...

Breathe in and out, in and out, slowly and without force...Breathe in and out 20 times...focusing your attention on the breath and removing the disturbing thoughts and stressful attitudes that may have disrupted your sleep the night before. They are gone. It is a new day and a fresh start for your life. Be grateful for this new beginning and vow to make the most of enjoying this day, moment to moment. Breathe in and out...inhaling the life force of the universe and exhaling away the worries and cares of the night before...

This is your time for solitude...a time to replenish your soul with the life force around you...the kind and benevolent force that brings joy into our hearts. If you allow this force into your life, you will find a universal and loving flow to your days—each breath brings in energy and throws off negativity—cleanse your mind and soul just as you cleanse your body daily...

Continue to breathe and remove all thoughts and worries from your mind. Instead of disturbing, black thought, visualize a bright, white light over your head, filtering down through your mind and into your spine. Let the light bathe and relax your forehead and remove the tension in your facial muscles...

Let your forehead relax...feel the muscles loosen as you give your forehead full attention...it is now smooth, calm and unfurrowed. Next, relax your cheek muscles and your jaw...feel your jaw get heavy as the muscles let go of their tension.

▼ ▼ ▼

Relax your lips, feel the space of air between them as the muscles relax and let go…

Now, follow the white light of bliss as it travels down your neck into your shoulders…feel the light warm the tight muscles of your neck and shoulders and help them relax and release their tension…feel the light work its way from the top of your spine down your shoulders and into your upper arms, relaxing your muscles as it travels its path. Relax your elbows and lower arms and wiggle your fingers slightly before letting them fall into a state of relaxation…

Feel your upper back relax as you bring the peace and calm of the universal life force into those tense muscles…feel the light give your muscles an internal massage, gently melting away the stress and tension that settles in your lower back, at the base of your spine…

Next, direct your attention to your stomach and breathe deeply to relax the muscles surrounding it. Much stress is contained here. Use the white light to bathe your stomach, cleansing it of tension and stress…undo the knots in your intestinal tract one by one, allowing the white light to travel freely throughout your internal organs…

If stressful thoughts about work or family make their way into your meditative space, gently brush them aside and continue relaxing your body…

Let your attention travel down your body to your loins. Relax your buttocks and your thighs, giving in to the force of gravity. Let your body sink into the ground, becoming one with the earth underneath…

Breathe deeply and relax your knees, letting them fall deeper into the ground below. Relax your calves and hamstrings, the muscles in front and back of your lower leg, letting them become soft and supple…

Focus your attention on your feet, your ankles and your toes…feel your heels relax and see the white light travel up the arch of each foot, to the balls of your feet and into your big

▼ ▼ ▼

toes…let the light work its way up and down each toe, until your feet feel heavy and fully relaxed…

Mentally scan your entire body, searching for signs of tension. Wherever you find it, send the white light into that area and let go, releasing the tension with your out-breath and bringing new energy into your body as you inhale.

When your body is totally relaxed, concentrate on your breathing once more. Breathe deeply, filling your lungs with life-giving oxygen and spiritual peace. Breathe in and out for 20 more counts…

Think of all the blessings you do have…your family and loved ones, and dedicate your meditation to them, wishing them the same peace and serenity you have achieved. Vow to remember this peaceful feeling throughout the day whenever you feel tension and stress building up. Place in your mind's eye the picture of a calm and serene you. Keep this mental picture ready should anxiety and aggravation creep into your life during the day…

See the white light flooding your entire being with peace and tranquility and awaken with optimism and the desire to share this wonderful feeling with others you may encounter on your day's journey.

Take 20 more deep breaths, then slowly lift your arms overhead and reach as high as you can, letting your shoulder muscles sink into gravity. Lower your chin to your chest for a moment and feel the tension release from your upper spine…stretch out your legs, allowing the flow of life-giving blood to enter every muscle and pore. Now begin to slowly rise, supporting your body with your hands, until you reach a standing position. Stretch skyward once more and bring your arms overhead…take a final lung-filling breath and bring your arms down to your sides. You are ready to begin a new day.

▼ ▼ ▼

2. EVENING MEDITATION

The evening meditation is essential for helping you unwind and preparing your mind for a peaceful night's rest. Take time out for yourself every night to repeat or listen to the following meditation, giving thanks for the bounty you received during the day and putting aside any problems until you are ready to tackle them refreshed the next morning.

Sit up on the edge of your bed or do this meditation lying down. If you are lying down, remove your pillow and lay your head flat on the bed. Let your arms fall loosely beside you. Breathe in and out at your own pace.

Focus your attention on the farthest tip of your nose, watching your nostril expand and contract with each breath. Continue to breathe, releasing negative energy and thoughts as you exhale and inhaling new energy and peace.

Feel your breath fill every part of your body. Feel the life force enter your brain and travel down through your spine, expanding to fill every organ, every muscle, every cell of your being.

Now picture yourself lying on the beach at the edge of the ocean. The sand is soft and soothing beneath your body. The air is fresh and pure. Smell the salt air as it enters your nostrils. Feel the breeze from the ocean as it bathes your body with serenity.

Listen to the sounds of the sea as you continue to breathe deeply in…and out…

Visualize in your mind's eye waves washing out to sea. With each wave, send a piece of your stress and tension…let the waves chip away at your stress, bit by bit, washing away the tension and leaving you relaxed and calm…

Picture your cares and worries like footsteps on the sand being washed away with each breath, with each wave…let your body flow with the tide as the waves cleanse negative thoughts from your mind…let your tension dissolve like footsteps in the sand with the waves that flow through your mind's eye…

▼ ▼ ▼

Focus your attention on your head and neck…let the waves wash away the tension in your face and neck…feel the tension float away from your shoulders and arms. Clench your fingers into a fist and then release…feel the stress leaving your arms through your fingertips…

Bring your attention to your stomach and internal organs…take a deep, deep breath filling your lungs and then your stomach with relaxing air…slowly exhale, letting all remaining tension in your body leave with this out breath…

Feel the waves wash away the tension and stress in the muscles of your legs…feel the peace and calm reach your feet and toes. Wriggle your toes one at a time and focus your attention on each one as you consciously and willfully relax one toe at a time…

Now breathe in deeply once more, filling your body with life-giving oxygen and pushing away the last vestiges of stress…repeat this breath 20 times, counting slowly to yourself…let the waves of your own breathing transport every bit of tension out of your body, leaving you relaxed and calm. Slowly stretch your arms above your head and feel the renewed peace and energy flow throughout your body…

Open your eyes and ever so slowly sit up and reach for your toes, relaxing your shoulder muscles as you stretch…sit up tall and breathe deeply five times…you are now calm, relaxed and focused. Have a wonderful night's sleep…

BREATHING EXERCISES

Your breath can be an instant tranquilizer. By learning how to use your breath to release stress, you have a portable escape hatch wherever and whenever you need help.

Deep and rhythmic breathing helps control inner tension and regulates your stress response. Taking a deep breath before making an important move or decision is an age-old way to help prepare and calm you down for the task ahead.

▼ ▼ ▼

To get the full benefits of deep breathing, try this method when you're alone:

1. Stand tall, feet together, shoulders back, and clasp your hands together, placing them under your chin. Now take a really deep breath to the count of six, bringing your elbows up as you inhale.

Leave your hands under your chin and push up slightly so your head is tilted backward. Continue raising your elbows, framing your face as you breathe in. Hold this breath for six more counts and then exhale to the count of six, bringing your elbows back to their original position, parallel to the ground. Your elbows act like bellows, helping to expand and contract the air in your lungs. Keep your shoulders down and relaxed.

Repeat this sequence 20 times.

▼ ▼ ▼

2. To detoxify your body and get rid of stressful poisons, sit on your knees, keeping your upper body tall and straight, hands on your knees in front of you.

Now, without inhaling, expel your breath in short, sharp sounds that resemble the word, "Shhh!" Use your stomach muscles to force out the air as you repeat "Shhh!" 35 times.

Return to normal breathing.

3. Lie on your back, feet comfortably apart and arms by your side. Inhale, through your nose, slowly to the count of eight. Hold your breath four counts and now slowly, through your mouth, exhale to the count of eight. Push every bit of air from your stomach when you exhale and fill every cavity of your lungs and stomach when you inhale.

Repeat 20 times. Return to normal breathing.

Once you are comfortable with the concept of deep, rhythmic breathing, use this technique as an instant stress-buster whenever you feel the onset of tension.

Practice at your desk. Practice on your break or lunch hour. Use your breath to melt away stress anytime. It's the most wondrous, natural stress-buster you can find.

VISUALIZATION

I used to chuckle when I read how-to books that encouraged you to picture what you wanted or how you wanted to look in order to obtain your goals. I thought it was ludicrous to imagine that visualizing your dreams could make them come true.

However, in my journey to find inner peace and self-discovery, I've found that visualization plays an extremely important role in creating the kind of life you want to live.

One of my mentors, Robbyn Muse, a delightful and agile yoga-meditation teacher, always ends her hatha yoga sessions with a 15-minute meditation using taped affirmations.

▼ ▼ ▼

Again, at first, my doubting mind balked at phrases like, "You are perfect the way you are," "You are happy and calm," or "You deserve to be wealthy so that you can celebrate life and share with others."

But the bottom line is, if you don't see, believe and integrate your own wishes in your own mind, you can't realize them. I recall that old adage, "Don't wish for something hard enough—you might just get it." I believe this to be true. I believe that if you picture yourself calm, and create a serene life in your own mind, you are one step closer to making this perception a reality.

On a recent Oprah Winfrey television program, her guest, Dr. Deepak Chopra, showed how visualization can actually destroy or mend our bodies. He explained how our thought processes determine the negative or positive flow of immunological messages throughout the central nervous system.

I was surprised when he said we basically have only two emotions: pain or pleasure. When we deny pain, we become angry or frustrated and sink into the realm of stress that destroys our bodies. In other words, it's better to deal with confrontations than avoid them. If you are sad, feel the sadness. Don't rely on pills, drugs, exercise or other means to temporarily shove that feeling aside. Feel your emotions, let them run their natural course, then go on with your life. The Australians, if you recall the film *Crocodile Dundee*, call this a "walkabout"—taking a respite from decisions and problems until you feel strong enough to deal with them.

When we operate out of stress, we don't make the right moves. We get in our own way. When we operate from a position of strength, or pleasure, our bodies sing to a different tune. We carry the notes with authority, and do not create discord within our own bodies and with others around us.

According to Chopra, and many longevity experts, we should easily live to at least 130 years of age if we learn to

▼ ▼ ▼

tune in to our pleasure center and take care of our thoughts which in turn take care of our body's aging mechanism.

Take the time to see yourself as a positive, loving and centered individual. See those around you bathed in a light of love. Refuse to see the black side of this world and you'll be rewarded with visions of beauty.

Use visualization to give yourself mini-vacations throughout the day. When you are ready to explode at your boss, take a step back and picture yourself totally in control of the situation. If you feel like the world is overwhelming you with problems, visualize yourself in command and tackle only one situation at a time. Or, take time out altogether and take a long leisurely walk. The problems will probably still be there waiting for you—but you'll be in a much better frame of mind to deal with them.

If there is something about your appearance—your weight, perhaps—you don't like, visualize yourself as you'd like to be. Picture yourself thinner or heavier; taller or shorter. You'll actually send out subconscious messages to those around you and will be viewed in a different manner. I've seen this work many times. I know some "short" folks who have so much self-esteem they give the impression of being ten feet tall!

Teach your children to use visualization instead of their fists to help solve their problems. Athletes have long used this technique to pitch the perfect throw, serve the perfect ace or swim with style and grace. If your child is having trouble dealing with a bully at school, teach him to picture the offender as a small, helpless child. We all know bullies who have backed down once confronted. If you are having a difficult time grasping a concept, see yourself calmly finding the solution. Give yourself the inner confidence to face life head on. Visualization helps give us a different perspective. We see obstacles as challenges, problems as ways to find solutions.

Since I have begun using visualization as an adjunct to my stress-busting program, I've found it a most valuable tool.

▼ ▼ ▼

When the day's chores seem to overpower me, I literally picture myself sailing through deadlines, housework and the like! When I'm having an ugly day—similar to a bad-hair day but ultimately all consuming—I'm able to look in the mirror and smile away the negative image.

Remember that old saying: "Beauty is in the eyes of the beholder." Use your inner eye to find beauty and peace in your life.

▼ ▼ ▼

Chapter Four

PERSONAL STRESS-BUSTING
STRATEGIES

Here's a delightful passage written by an 85-year-old woman reflecting on the missed years of her life. Nadine Stair penned this famous passage to remind us that life can pass by far too quickly if we don't learn to focus in on today. Living for tomorrow not only produces stress, it short-changes us on the joys of the present.

How I'd Live My Life Again
Nadine Stair

I'd like to make more mistakes next time. I'd relax. I would limber up. I would be sillier than I have been this trip. I would take fewer things seriously. I would take more chances. I would climb more mountains and swim more rivers. I would eat more ice cream and less beans. I would perhaps have more actual troubles but I'd have fewer imaginary ones.

▼ ▼ ▼

You see, I am one of those people who live sensibly and sanely hour after hour, day after day. Oh, I've had my moments, and if I had to do it over again, I'd have more of them. In fact, I'd try to have nothing else. Just moments, one after another, instead of living so many years ahead of each day. I've been one of those persons who never goes anywhere without a thermometer, a hot-water bottle, a raincoat, and a parachute.

If I had to do it again, I would travel lighter than I have. If I had my life to live over again, I would start barefoot earlier in the spring and stay that way later in the fall. I would go to more dances. I would ride more merry-go-rounds. I would pick more daisies.

Stress-busting strategies should be geared to your individual personality. As Dr. Selye pointed out, some of us are "racehorses" who operate better in a highly challenging enviroment. Others are "turtles" and need a slower, more regulated pace.

Neither personality type is "good" nor "bad." If we recall the famous fable by Aesop that described the race between the tortoise and the hare, we know that it was indeed the slower moving tortoise who made it to the finish line first.

There are many of us who fluctuate between the two types.

We can work like crazy for a period of time and then collapse into lethargy. We need time to recharge our batteries before we rejoin the racehorse crowd.

Different personalities need different ways to cope with stress. For example, for the tortoise, a yearly vacation is more desirable than frequent breaks.

The tortoise may choose to spend a vacation at a fishing resort, leisurely enjoying nature at its own pace. The racehorse on the other hand, would benefit from shorter breaks timed on a more frequent basis. This personality might thrive on an action-packed vacation spent skydiving.

The tortoise might use yoga or a less intense exercise program to de-stress. The racehorse would jump for joy at a

▼　▼　▼

high-impact aerobic exercise class or choose jogging to relieve stress. But surprisingly, both types should experiment with stress-busting strategies that are entirely opposite to their personality types. The turtle might find a more energetic hobby exciting and highly rewarding. The super-charged racehorse might become enamored with yoga and meditation -once he or she stays still long enough to enjoy it.

That's why it is so important to develop your own personalized stress-busting plan. Socrates advised his disciples to "Know Thyself." These two simple words sum up the real secret to leading a happy, stress-free life. Take the time to really get to know yourself and discover the best techniques to remove stress from your life. It may take some trial and error, but if you don't try—and don't err—you'll never learn to wear the lifestyle that suits you best.

DEALING WITH WORK PRESSURES

Job stress is a worldwide plague that afflicts everyone from waitresses to executives, according to a 1993 United Nations report.

"Stress has become one of the most serious health issues of the 20th century," says the World Labor Report by the U.N.'s International Labor Organization.

The report calls job stress a "global phenomenon."

In the United States, one study reveals that stress-related diseases such as ulcers, high blood pressure and heart attacks cost the U.S. economy $200 billion a year in absenteeism, compensation claims and medical expenses.

Stress stems from impersonal, ever-changing and even hostile workplaces, but the U.N. report says workers can deal with stress through relaxation exercises, diet, counseling and changing their attitudes and behavior.

The Reverend Richard Dortch, former president of the PTL (Praise the Lord) ministry, now operates the Life Challenge workshops in Largo, Florida. He counsels profes-

▼ ▼ ▼

sional men who have lost sight of their path and are deeply troubled by stress.

"Men's stress stems mostly from the search for self-identity," he says. "They forget to balance their professional lives with family life, hobbies and the many other elements that establish their identity."

His advice applies, of course, to both men and women who are caught up in high-powered, aggressive careers. Always remember that you are not your job. You work at your job, and hopefully, love your work. Keep work problems in perspective and don't let pressures "get to you."

Keep small momentos of your family life—photos, a child's crayon drawing or another keepsake—in full view so that when you find yourself becoming overwhelmed and carried away by on-the-job stress, you can take a mental break to achieve balance and perspective.

When you leave work for the day, make the transition from job to home a little smoother by:

- Giving yourself a break. Cut your lunch hour if you have to and leave work early to beat the traffic and get home early for a change.
- Using your mind's eye to make the mental transition from work to home a happy one. Visualization is a powerful tool.
- Understanding that children are children and it's their nature to be raucous and demanding. Exercise benevolent patience when they vie for your love and attention.
- Forgetting your own tiredness and focusing on the love your family is extending. Give each member a special time.
- Preparing dinner for the most part in the morning so you don't have to rush into the kitchen as soon as you arrive home. Have the whole family pitch in to prepare the evening meal while you nibble on healthy snacks such as raw vegetables. It's a great time to unwind and talk.

▼ ▼ ▼

- Going for a walk together before dinner. While the stew is simmering or the chicken baking, take a half-hour stroll. The fresh air and exercise help reduce stress.
- Taking a hot shower and changing into your "evening" clothes. Whether it's a pair of shorts or old baggy jeans, get comfortable.
- Giving your spouse a special hug. Bring home flowers every now and then—for no special reason.
- Arranging a dinner date with your mate—just the two of you—as often as you feel the need. You don't have to spend big bucks to enjoy this treat, either. Pack a picnic and enjoy a park repast.

FAMILY STRESS

Many of us can trace the source of our stress directly to conflicts within the home unit. Here's an interesting quiz that helps pinpoint the source of your family's stress triggers.

Answer YES or NO to the chores you personally attend to the majority of the time.

▼ ▼ ▼

1. Housework
2. Food and clothing shopping
3. Paying bills
4. Cooking
5. Taking care of homework and school projects
6. Planning and decorating
7. Planning social activities
8. Supervising and disciplining the children
9. Taking care of dental and medical appointments
10. Scheduling repairs and maintenance

Review the quiz and see where you can share or delegate some of the responsibility to other members of the household.

Now take the following quiz which determines the quality of time you actually spend with your family. Which of the following categories do you feel need improvement? Where would you rather spend your time and energy?

1. Personal recreation
2. Talking with your spouse
3. Having fun with your children
4. Making love
5. Relaxing with personal projects and hobbies
6. Listening to your family's concerns and problems
7. Planning for the future
8. Vacations
9. Going to movies and other family outings
10. Alone

If you are like most folks, you'd probably like to spend less time doing the activities in the first quiz and far more time enjoying the second categories.

So make your move! Trade some of your chores for more pleasurable activities starting today. The dust will wait. Your own personal satisfaction cannot. Learn to divide and conquer daily stressors by delegating duties to others.

Be patient and honest with your family. Help them learn to be responsible for their own cleanliness, clothes and per-

▼ ▼ ▼

sonal welfare. Do your children and spouse a favor by teaching them to be considerate and helpful.

Use your own mental power to make tedious tasks tolerable. For example, put on your favorite music as you dust or clean and train yourself to enjoy this time moment by moment instead of dreading the work. As you're peeling those potatoes for supper, remember how lucky you are to have food on the table. Think of those less fortunate who are starving and would give their eye teeth for the pleasure of peeling potatoes!

Exercise your rights as a parent. Too many working moms and dads try to alleviate their sense of "guilt" by allowing their offspring to walk all over them. Don't fall into this trap. You have the right to peace and quiet. You have the right to their respectful behavior and co-operation.

Children need discipline and are much happier when they have limits to follow. You are working for their welfare as well as your own. Take a "tough love" stance today and you will be rewarded with thankful, caring children tomorrow.

HOLIDAY STRESS

It seems stress levels skyrocket during the so-called Happy Holiday season. What should be a time of joy while gathering friends and family together often erupts into arguments, overdrawn bank accounts and credit cards exceeding their limits.

It doesn't have to be this way. You can return to the true meaning of your religious season by shedding the phoniness once and for all and getting back to basics.

Many families have decided to set limits on gift expenditures to ease the financial burden. Be direct with your family and tell them in advance that you will be spending, say, $10 a gift this year. Even better, if you have a hobby or craft that you enjoy, encourage family members to make their own gifts to share.

▼ ▼ ▼

Children can color pictures of themselves or your immediate family to be circulated to distant relatives as gifts. You can create a photo montage of annual events such as birthdays and anniversaries and send them to people afar. Personal, meaningful presents are ultimately more valuable than store-bought items.

Avoid unrealistic expectations at holiday gatherings. Statistics show that few Americans actually look forward to family dinners because of the fussing and feuding that usually takes place. Indeed, holiday get-togethers can be—and often are—disasters. Uncle Pete and Aunt Martha insist on arguing throughout the meal. Your mother treats you like a two-year-old in front of your own children and your father does nothing but criticize.

You come away feeling stuffed from eating too much, depressed from expecting too much and lonelier than ever. If this scenario sounds familiar, it's time for a change. You've got several choices. First, alter your thinking and vow not to let family members get under your skin. They can't upset you unless you give them permission. Detach yourself from their words and actions and make the most out of the occasion.

Second, be honest with yourself and family. If someone does say something hurtful let him know. Confront the person and say, "That was a cruel remark and I don't wish to hear it again."

If you take a firm stand, the aggressor will usually back down. Very often people do not realize how cutting their remarks can be and are cruel out of habit.

Third, if all else fails, stay away. There's no point in beating yourself up for the sake of an arbitrary holiday. Celebrate good times alone with your spouse or a close friend…or even alone, if necessary. I've spent several Christmases by myself. The first one, admittedly, was rotten. I felt sorry for myself all day.

However, once I trained myself to do positive, pleasant tasks during this day, I completely changed my holiday feeling

▼ ▼ ▼

into one of joy. I volunteered in soup kitchens for several years, serving turkey dinners to the homeless. It was a wonderful way to spend the holidays! You really learn to count your blessings when you see so many people worse off than you.

Now that I have remarried, my husband and I spend our holidays together—just the two of us and our four four-legged beasties. I do make traditional fare and we enjoy lots of leftovers with little or no cooking for days on end.

We came to terms with the fact that we love our families dearly—but from afar. We stopped attending family gatherings because of the tension and stress. It wasn't as difficult as it sounds! In fact, we're closer to our families now than ever before. Perhaps absence does make the heart grow fonder!

Protecting your own feelings by staying clear of hurtful people is not confrontational. It's often the only way you can develop a truly productive relationship with your family. You *can* turn holiday stress around by taking control and regaining the joy seasonal celebrations should bring to your heart.

STRESS THROUGH ISOLATION

It's no secret that in this society, the extended family unit has been replaced by millions of people fending alone for themselves. Without the support system of loving relatives, many people suffer from the stress of loneliness.

When you are alone—and lonely—you tend to focus on the bugaboos, the problems of everyday life. However, living alone doesn't mean that you must be lonely.

There are plenty of single folks who lead happy and productive lives and who are not in the least bit lonely. They may occasionally miss steady companionship, but they have learned to depend on their own resources for inner joy.

For life to be fulfilling, you must help yourself to its nourishment. Reach out and make your own waves so the tide of love and purpose may return to your life. Get out and meet

▼ ▼ ▼

people. Find and develop a hobby. Go back to school. Renew an old interest. Volunteer your services in the community.

These are just some of the ways you can put yourself back into the mainstream of life instead of remaining self-focused and isolated. It may be difficult in the beginning, if you are accustomed to being independent and alone, but once you break through the barrier of fear and insecurity, you'll find many rewards awaiting you.

It's never too late to start exploring new horizons. Check your local newspaper for the calendar of events. You'll find listings for every age and taste. Call your community center or YMCA for advice. If you belong to a church or synagogue, ask to be put in touch with families who may need your loving assistance.

But if you don't find what you need there, start your own group! Place an ad explaining that you want to form a discussion or reading group, begin a knitting circle or help a single parent with her children a few afternoons a week.

Visit your Humane Society and help care for the animals on hand if you cannot have one of your own. I cannot emphasize strongly enough how

▼ ▼ ▼

much a four-footed, finned or feathered friend can add joy and purpose to your life.

Many people who live alone would wither and die if not for their animal companions. They need all that love you've got bottled up inside and they will reward you a thousand-fold with affection.

Don't let yourself fall into the rut of self-pity and despair because you are alone. If you don't reach out, you'll never grasp a helping hand.

DEALING WITH LIFE'S EVERYDAY STRESS

Your stress may come from many different sources. In order to deal with the many little annoyances that can snow-ball into giant stressors, develop different "time-out" strategies to help you regain the perspective you need to better deal efficiently with issues.

We've all had moments when we felt so out of control that it was impossible to make a rational decision. At those times it is almost impossible to meditate or even exercise the stress away because we are so overwhelmed and confused.

Once again, you can train your mind to overcome those stressful hurdles by using a few tricks:

- Remind yourself that the stressor will disappear in time and you will barely remember the feeling of frustration it created.
- Ask yourself if whatever is causing your stress would be as important if you had only one day to live.
- Talk about the problem with someone whose judgment you trust.
- Get a therapeutic massage. To me, there is nothing more relaxing and mentally revitalizing than a massage. Let someone's healing hands remove your tension.
- If you are upset or angry at the way you've been talked to or treated by an individual, confront the person with your feelings. Perhaps you misread or misheard the true

▼ ▼ ▼

meaning of what was said or done. Taking direct action is often the simplest and best way to deal with a stressful situation.

- Retreat for as long as you need to regain your sense of emotional balance. I've got a miniature "altar" at home, a corner of my room filled with objects that spell serenity to me. There's a collection of photographs of loved ones, including one of me as a happy small child. I've placed several pictures and statues of religious significance on my "altar." These provide an oasis of serenity when daily life seems too much to take.
- Listening to your favorite soothing music can also provide quick relief. Music can soothe the savage breast, so keep a few relaxing tapes on hand to help de-stress your day. Classical music, ballads or even tapes of nature's sounds are wonderful.
- Take a hike. Go for a long, long walk and don't come back until you feel better.

GET OFF THE MERRY-GO-ROUND

A charming old fellow I met while camping in the Northeast Georgia mountains took pleasure in regaling me with a few funny stories about the city folk who descend upon his campground each weekend.

Bill Rector, a slow-talking, pipe-smoking gentleman of indeterminate years, gave up the "good life," a corporate job, a fine house in Florida and the accouterments surrounding his success to work and live in the Georgia wilds.

He lives out of his camper, sharing food and camaraderie with visitors—many of whom are of the opposite sex. Bill may not have a lot of money or power, but he's definitely king of the hill in his neck of the woods!

"Folks come up here and tell me how they envy my life," he confides with a knowing wink. "They go on and on about how they'd love to do what I do: git up in the mornin',

▼ ▼ ▼

shower in the crik, and eat a mighty fine breakfast slow-cooked over a camp stove.

"And I listen to 'em and I know down deep they really don't want to give up them fancy houses nor those fast-movin' cars they speed down the highway.

"You see, the diff'rence 'tween them and me is I like who I am...I like where I am...and I ain't in no hurry to git someplace diff'rent.

"I don't keep up with those proverbial Joneses who have a lot of nice, new stuff. And if the Joneses would quit eatin' that expensive junk food and tradin' cars every year they might have a few dollars in the bank. If you was really serious about gittin' off that treadmill, you'd figure out a way to slow down so it'd be safe to git off.

"Don't envy me," Bill says shaking his head. "I ain't so smart. But I ain't dumb enough to let car salesmen, credit card companies, bankers and pizza parlor folks outsmart me every time I turn around.

"And don't tell me you ain't got enough time to slow down and take the kids campin' 'cause you've got to pay for their

▼ ▼ ▼

fancy education and the like. There ain't no finer education than spendin' time with your kids, learnin' about nature and being calm."

As Pine Knot would say, "Nuff said!"

▼ ▼ ▼

Chapter Five

STRESS-BUSTING
DIET PLAN

You are what you eat…and if you fill your body with junk food, your mental balance will be garbage as well. You cannot expect to maintain a calm and controlled attitude when your poor, nutritionally starved body is busy fighting fat and lethargy.

The more you consume highly processed foods, the more your system must fight to stay healthy. And that fight depletes not only your immune system, but your stress-busting ability as well.

Most of us don't reach for healthy carrot sticks or low-fat muffins when we're stressed out. Instead, we gravitate to so-called "comfort foods" like ice cream, chocolate chip cookies and other fat-sweet combination treats to soothe our souls.

We revert to the foods we had as kids to take away the pain of adult stress and responsibility. But experts warn that

▼ ▼ ▼

avoiding stress by sinking our teeth into rich, fatty foods only aggravates the situation.

Dr. Judith Wurtman has done extensive research on foods that affect your mood. She's found that low-fat, high protein foods rev up your system while foods that are calming tend to be those rich in complex carbohydrates.

Carbohydrates, eaten alone, boost your brain's serotonin levels. Serotonin is the chemical that soothes your body's tension and helps you relax. Protein foods, on the other hand— meats, dairy and fish—squelch serotonin and help boost your brain power. By eating the right kinds of food at the right times throughout the day, you can avoid too many highs and lows in your mood and energy levels. You can also boost your brain power and remain focused on the task at hand instead of scattering your energies in a thousand different directions.

Keeping your body and mind well fueled with just the right kind of food helps you maintain the balance necessary to prevent stress buildup. That's why it's important to prepare a game plan designed to help you avoid eating the wrong, high-calorie foods that will not only make you sluggish and unable to focus—they'll make you fat!

When you are filled with tension and stress, eat something calming like a baked potato or air-popped corn—without adding loads of toppings or butter. When you need to be sharp and focused, eat a piece of low-fat cheese or an ounce of lean meat or poultry.

Here are some more excellent stress-busting foods:

- Pasta with steamed vegetables and marinara sauce
- low-salt pretzels
- steamed rice and veggies
- pancakes with low-fat syrup
- pita pocketbread with sliced tomatoes and lettuce
- baked potatoes topped with steamed spinach
- graham or animal crackers
- low-fat muffins

▼ ▼ ▼

- low-fat frozen yogurt or sherbet

Drinking soothing herbal teas, especially chamomile, is a proven way to reduce stress. You can use a little sugar to sweeten the tea or spice it up with cinnamon or lemon juice.

JOYFUL JUICES

The best stress-busting nutritional investment you can make is to buy a juicer. I discovered the joys of juicing from veteran body builder Jack Lalanne, who is at the peak of physical and mental condition in his late 70's. Both he and his adorable wife, Elaine, drink loads of fresh vegetable juice every day to supplement a healthful, low-fat diet. They also exercise regularly and are in remarkable shape as a result.

This dynamic couple are living proof how stress-busting foods and a solid, healthy lifestyle improve your physical and mental capacities. They both work a schedule that would leave most of us gasping for breath!

I have a juicer that not only prepares the most delicious natural juices but can also make homemade nut butters and homogenized fruit ices to rival the best gourmet ice creams.

When I need a quick and inexpensive pick-me-up, I make the following juice out of chilled, fresh veggies:

4 scraped carrots
2 stalks celery (leaves included)
1/4 beet

I blend and drink the juice immediately. No matter how tired or stressed out I feel beforehand, I invariably feel revitalized moments after downing this blend.

You can vary the basic recipe by adding apples, spinach, kale, fresh oranges or other seasonal produce.

And when I want a real stress-soothing snack, I make the following iced fruit mixture that I swear is creamier and far more refreshing than any commercially prepared frozen treat.

▼ ▼ ▼

Homogenized, frozen fruit blends are extremely nutritious and fat-free. Here's the basic recipe for one serving:

1 frozen banana
3 frozen strawberries
1/4 cup frozen blueberries

Mix the above in your juicer and drink right away. You can freeze the mixture for a short while, but after an hour or so, ice crystals form and you may want to reblend the fruit cream again to make it more palatable.

You can also add frozen pineapple, peaches or other sliced fruit in season. Make sure all ingredients are frozen, however, for the best results. I normally buy over-ripe bananas on sale at my supermarket. Peel them and freeze them in halves in a plastic storage bag for instant use.

Fresh fruit juice is also a real treat. Watermelon, in season, makes an excellent drink that's cheap and rich in nutrients.

Speaking of fresh veggies and juices, try using them topically to reduce stress, too. Sliced cucumbers are super for reducing facial tension. Lie down and place thinly sliced cucumbers on each eyelid. You'll feel refreshed instantly. Lemon juice makes an excellent skin toner. Rub a little lemon juice on your elbows and knees to soften and smooth the skin.

MORE FOODS TO BEAT STRESS

Avoid alcohol when you're feeling depressed. There's nothing wrong with a cocktail or wine with your meal on occasion, but don't use booze to beat stress, because it will dispirit you further, exaggerating your depression to a rock bottom low.

If you're tempted to down that martini to banish stress, take a walk instead, and postpone the drink until you're feeling more relaxed.

▼ ▼ ▼

Eating nutritiously definitely helps beat stress. When your body is getting adequate nutrients, you tend to cope with life in a more positive way. Quite frankly, this is simply common sense, but we tend to forget that food is our body's source of fuel. As functioning human beings we require more than pre-packaged mixes designed for quick and easy eating to nourish our bodies. Think about what you put into your mouth. Read labels. If you can't pronounce an ingredient, chances are you won't want it in your body!

Choose foods that are nutrient dense. This means that ounce for ounce, calorie for calorie, you should select your menu from the richest sources of vitamins and minerals. Unfortunately, most fast and frozen foods just don't make the grade. The more a food has been prepared and processed, the fewer nutrients remain. For example, the nutrients in canned goods amount to only 30 percent of the nutrients in the same food in its raw state.

Once you embark upon a healthy eating plan, you'll find that you feel stronger and more able to cope with life's stress. You'll also have more energy and in all likelihood, drop those extra pounds you've been trying to lose.

Here's a sample of a stress-busting eating plan to help you get started. It's not a weight-reducing plan, but most folks will lose weight in spite of themselves because the menu includes top-quality foods to help balance your body's metabolism and burn calories faster and more efficiently.

You do not have to eat the different breakfasts and lunches as they are mentioned. Some of us are content to consume the same meals almost every day. For example, I eat a fresh orange or grapefruit with a slice of bread or bagel and cottage cheese every morning for breakfast.

It may sound boring, but I prefer not having to think about preparing meals that early in the morning!

For lunch, I stick to low-fat frozen yogurt or a pita-pocket tomato sandwich. These menu suggestions illustrate how you

▼ ▼ ▼

can mix and match stress-busting foods at various times of the day.

With this diet plan, you certainly won't be hungry. The problem with most stress-based eaters is they starve themselves all day then become out-of-control eaters at night. By eating right, and consuming the majority of your nutrients throughout the day, you'll avoid dangerous night-time binging.

Day 1

BREAKFAST: 1 small orange; 1 slice 7-grain bread; 1/4 cup low-fat cottage cheese; a little fruit jelly.

MID-MORNING SNACK: 1 apple.

LUNCH: 1 cup vegetable soup with 4 rye crackers; chopped egg sandwich on whole-wheat bread or toast.

MID-AFTERNOON SNACK: 1 cup low-fat yogurt.

SUPPER: Plate of spaghetti with marinara sauce; 1 cup steamed broccoli and mushrooms; small dinner salad with low-fat dressing.

EVENING SNACK: Herbal tea with low-fat muffin.

Day 2

BREAKFAST: 1 cup cantaloupe balls; 1 toasted bagel with sugar-free jelly.

MID-MORNING SNACK: 1 hard-boiled egg.

LUNCH: 1 2-ounce roast beef sandwich on rye; 1 apple.

MID-AFTERNOON SNACK: 1 ounce cheese with 10 grapes.

SUPPER: 1 baked potato topped with low-fat sour cream; 1 cup steamed spinach; 1 cup carrot coins, steamed; small dinner salad with low-fat dressing.

EVENING SNACK: 1 cup low-fat yogurt.

Day 3

BREAKFAST: 1 cup bran cereal with chopped fruit; 1/2 cup low-fat milk.

MID-MORNING SNACK: 1 banana.

LUNCH: Large fruit plate on lettuce; 1 slice French bread.

MID-AFTERNOON SNACK: 2 slices turkey breast; 4 crackers.

SUPPER: Chinese stir-fry with 4 ounces lean beef, 1 cup broccoli and 1 cup sliced mushrooms on rice.

EVENING SNACK: 1 cup air-popped corn.

Day 4

BREAKFAST: 1/2 cup grapefruit juice; 1 scrambled egg; 2 slices whole-wheat toast.

MID-MORNING SNACK: 1 pear.

LUNCH: 2 ounces sliced low-fat cheese melted in a pita pocket; 1 sliced tomato; 1 peach.

MID-AFTERNOON SNACK: 1 cup air-popped corn.

SUPPER: 4 ounces broiled salmon steak; 1 cup asparagus, steamed; 1 cup brown rice.

EVENING SNACK: 1 cup low-fat frozen yogurt.

Day 5

BREAKFAST: 1 cup berries; 1/2 cup oatmeal; 1/2 cup skim milk.

MID-MORNING SNACK: 1 ounce hard cheese; 4 crackers.

LUNCH: Shrimp salad with lettuce, tomatoes and cucumbers.

MID-AFTERNOON SNACK: 1 apple.

▼ ▼ ▼

SUPPER: 2 slices cheese pizza; small dinner salad with low-fat dressing.

EVENING SNACK: 1 banana.

Day 6

BREAKFAST: 3 small pancakes topped with fresh or drained, water-packed sliced peaches.

MID-MORNING SNACK: 1 apple.

LUNCH: 4-ounce lean hamburger on whole grain bun; pickles and tomatoes; coleslaw.

MID-AFTERNOON SNACK: 1 cup low-fat yogurt.

SUPPER: Broiled chicken breast; 1 cup pasta with tomato sauce and low-fat grated cheese; 1 cup steamed green beans.

EVENING SNACK: small bunch grapes; 2 fat-free cookies.

Day 7

BREAKFAST OR BRUNCH: 1 cup fresh fruit; 2 slices bacon; 1 poached egg on a toasted English muffin.

LUNCH: 1 cup beef stew; 1 hard roll.

MID-AFTERNOON SNACK: 1 pear.

SUPPER: 3 slices roast turkey or chicken; 1 small roasted potato; 1 cup steamed cabbage and carrots.

EVENING SNACK: 1 baked apple with cinnamon and topped with low-fat yogurt.

To enhance the flavor of your food, try some of the many new varieties of fat-free salad dressings and toppings currently available on supermarket shelves. And don't limit the dressing to only greens.

Top salmon steaks with low-fat ranch or honey-mustard dressing before cooking. Toss left-over rice or pasta with garlic

▼ ▼ ▼

herb dressing to make a delicious cold pasta salad for the next day.

Marinate green beans or asparagus in Italian dressing and serve them raw. Or use blue cheese dressing on tomatoes to make a delicious side dish or sandwich filling and make sure you drink lots of pure water—at least eight glasses a day.

Convenience Foods Can Be Fine

We all resort to convenience foods when our schedules get hectic, and everyone's eating dinner at a different time. These days, thank goodness, there are healthful and tasty frozen foods available that are also low in fat and calories.

Choose frozen meals that have 325 calories or less, with at least 20 grams of protein, 15 grams of carbohydrate and no more than 8 grams of fat per serving. They should also contain less than 500 milligrams (mg) of sodium per serving.

Read labels carefully. I was nicely fooled the other day when buying a frozen lasagna dinner. The label on the 8-ounce brand I selected had all the correct "per serving" requirements. However, when I double-checked the label, it said that the dinner served two! That tiny portion of lasagna could in no way serve two people and its label contents were grossly misleading.

A similar 10-ounce frozen lasagna dinner by another company had the same nutrients per serving but correctly stated that the package served one. This was a true indication of the contents.

So watch your serving sizes when you buy convenience foods. That package of rice and broccoli may boast only 150 calories per serving, but if the package says it serves six, and you know the two of you will polish it off, you're really getting three times the amount of fat and calories per serving.

Fast-food chains are becoming increasingly aware of health choices. Arby's, Wendy's and McDonald's all have

▼ ▼ ▼

low-fat items on their menus that won't bog you down or make you sluggish.

Although I am not a fast-food fan, I also applaud McDonald's for introducing bagels, low-fat bran muffins, low-fat milk, frozen low-fat yogurt and lower fat burgers and fajitas to its menu.

RULE OF THUMB: ELIMINATE SUGARS AND FAT

To keep your body and mind healthy, learn to eat a fat-free, sugar-free diet. We can obtain enough natural fat and sugar from eating the variety of foods listed in the sample menu above.

I personally do not endorse using artificial sweeteners and other chemical substitutes for fat and sugar. I believe these are just teasers and that it's easier to re-train our taste buds to enjoy healthy, natural flavors than it is to mask good food with this goop.

I do recommend pan sprays, however, for frying and baking. These products save a lot of fat calories and certainly yield good results besides saving cleanup time. I use these sprays for indoor frying, baking and outdoor grilling almost every day.

Remember that you are in control of your eating habits. If you are a compulsive eater, especially under stress, you may want to seek counseling to help you find a better way to cope. Plus, there are many support groups that offer free advice. However, ultimately you must take charge of your own health and start feeding your body a healthy, stress-busting array of foods. You'll reap the rewards now and for the rest of your life.

Good nutrition is the best investment you can make not only for stress-busting, but also for building a strong body to carry you into the future.

▼ ▼ ▼

Chapter Six

STRESS AND

EXERCISE

Regular daily exercise is a wonderful way to reduce stress.

Setting aside an hour a day to work on your body is an easy way to improve both your mental and physical well-being.

The key to finding and enjoying a regular exercise program is selecting varied activities that are pleasing to your personality.

Your neighbor might thrive on driving, high-impact aerobic dance classes with lots of noise and loud, funky music. But this same type of class may be jarring and stressful to you. You may be better off taking hatha yoga or ballroom dancing instead.

I was a devoted aerobic dance enthusiast, attending classes almost daily. Although I usually enjoyed the endorphin "high" I would get after such vigorous exercise, there were many days when the workout was arduous and non-produc-

▼ ▼ ▼

tive. Instead of releasing tension and stress—the main reason for my endeavors—I felt tired and even more depressed.

Luckily, a highly qualified yoga teacher joined the staff of my exercise studio and I rediscovered the joys of this ancient form of exercise.

Celeste was a ballerina who turned to hatha or physical yoga to reduce the stress in her life. She practice what is called the Bikram method of yogic exercise, a series of methodically planned poses that completely revitalize and tone the body while providing a mighty cardiovascular workout. Many Hollywood celebrities take classes from the outspoken and often outrageous Bikram Choudry including Shirley Maclaine, Quincy Jones and John Saxon.

As soon as I added Celeste's classes to my exercise program, I felt much more centered and relaxed. Because I am essentially a racehorse in character, this focused and intense yoga workout is actually more effective in relieving my tension than social, outgoing forms of exercise.

Finding the right exercise program is really a matter of trial and error. You may choose from a variety of stress-reducing exercise programs ranging from walking to competitive sports. More and more women are discovering the advantages of weight training as a terrific tension-buster. Lifting those heavy weights takes a lot of effort and concentration. A 15-minute daily workout with heavy hands, rubber bands or free-weights for strength training relieves tension and stress from all your muscles, and also helps to burn fat calories and ward off osteoporosis.

It is important, however, to do some form of physical exercise *each* and *every day*. Since most of us have sedentary jobs, we just aren't using enough physical energy to balance the mental energy we're consuming. And that's how stress gets its head start.

While the experts say you can get away with three good 30-minute, aerobic workouts a week to build cardiovascular

▼ ▼ ▼

strength and endurance, I advise adding at least three more cross-training workouts to balance the stress-busting budget.

Brisk walking, weight training, yoga, martial arts, and competitive or social sports such as tennis and racquetball are all examples of alternative exercises.

Step-aerobics is also an excellent way to build cardiovascular strength without abusing the body. Avoid too many high-impact aerobic dance sessions unless you are very young and in great shape. Since the fitness industry has become smarter and more injury aware, the trend is definitely moving toward lower impact aerobics and away from bone-jarring, high-impact movements.

MAKE THE TIME

The excuse I hear from both men and women is:
"I don't have time to exercise! I'm busy enough as it is!"
There are 24 hours in the day. Allotting 10 of these for eating and sleeping and another 10 for working and commuting, still leaves us with a full four hours to fill.

Fit your workout schedule into the nooks and crannies in your day. Walk that extra block by getting to work a few minutes early. Do sit-ups while you're waiting for the chicken to cook. Ride your stationary bike or use the rowing machine while watching the late-night news. Climb the steps to the

▼ ▼ ▼

second or third floor of your office building instead of taking the elevator. Use your lunch hour to attend a nearby stretch-and-tone exercise class.

You may need to take a moment and write out a schedule at first to get the ball rolling. Having a printed schedule helps most of us see where time is slipping away and where we can fit in exercise.

HERE'S AN EXAMPLE:

6:30-7:00 a.m. Meditation
7:00-7:30 a.m. Breakfast and shower
7:30-8:30 a.m. Commute to work; walk a bit of the way
9:00-1:00 p.m. Work
1:00-2:00 p.m. Lunch; Take a 30-minute walk
2:00-5:00 p.m. Work
5:00-6:00 p.m. Commute home; walk a bit en route
6:15-7:00 p.m. Greet children, talk and prepare dinner
7:00-7:30 p.m. Eat dinner and do dishes
7:30-8:00 p.m. Take a long walk or do toning exercises
8:00-10:00 p.m. Television, reading or helping with homework
10:00-10:30 p.m. Meditation and relaxation exercises

As you can see, we've scheduled in quite a few exercise breaks that don't require lengthy commitments. If you can attend a regular exercise program at the Y or a health club, by all means do so. Make arrangements with your mate or a neighbor to watch the children so you can attend an evening or early morning session.

Many companies offer lunch-time workouts for their employees. To me, this is a great time of the day to use physical exercise to reduce stress. Many workers find themselves in a physical and mental slump after downing a heavy lunch. You'll be amazed how much sharper and less sluggish you'll feel on the job after a lunch-hour workout.

▼ ▼ ▼

CHOOSE THE ACTIVITY YOU LIKE BEST

You are more likely to stick with an exercise program if you select an activity that you truly enjoy. If you loved skating as a child, invest in a pair of ice or in-line skates. It won't take long to get back into the swing of things!

If swimming is your passion, find a local pool club you can join. Or try something completely different. For example, the martial arts provide excellent stress-reducing workouts as well as skill-building techniques and you might even have some fun.

My latest exercise craze is boxing! Thanks to my dynamic instructor, Billy Hodge, I've discovered the wonderful benefits of jumping rope, hitting that bag and learning to "bob and weave." Boxing is great for your body and is a superb stress-buster. After a few minutes of pounding the bag, you haven't an ounce of tension left in your entire being!

Get started now and develop a regular routine. There are times we'd all like to kick back and avoid exerting ourselves. There are times even changing into my exercise costume seems too big a chore. But, invariably, after all is said and done, you feel much better after a good, all-over workout.

And the benefits are long lasting. Scientific studies through the years have consistently shown that folks who engage in regular physical activity live longer and healthier and enjoy life more than those who don't.

RELAXATION EXERCISES

You can "spot reduce" stress by using the following instant relaxation exercises to remove tension from key trigger spots in the body.

▼ ▼ ▼

1. Stress has a tendency to collect in our neck and shoulder muscles when we're working or thinking too hard. For relief, lower you chin to your chest slowly and count to 10.

Now clasp your hands and stretch them, palms outward, in front of you. Stretch your hands as far away from your body as you can, feeling your shoulder and neck muscles lengthen. Pull your hands overhead and take that stretch as far back as you can. Hold for as long as you feel the need, then relax.

2. If you are stuck in a sedentary job, chances are you also get tense in your lower back. To help release stress in this area, lie on your back and bring your knees slowly, one at a time, to your chest. Hug them tightly and stay in this fetal position for at least one minute. Slowly bring your legs back down to the floor and repeat.

3. To help release tension throughout the body and recharge your mental batteries, the "ragdoll" is an excellent exercise. Stand tall, feet about 12 inches apart, and let your upper body flop forward, towards the floor, hanging like a ragdoll. Let your fingers touch the floor and sweep them slowly from side to side. Relax every muscle in your body. Slowly rise up. Your head is the last part of your body to come upright.

▼ ▼ ▼

Summary

▼ ▼ ▼ ▼

I recall reading a passage recently in which the author differentiated between a "human being" and a "human doing." We are human beings, put on this earth to live moment by moment one day at a time.

Unfortunately, we are caught up in a society of humans "doing." We always seem to be measured by our material accomplishments instead of inner worth. We're constantly on the go, trying to impress some unseen power with how great we are, how strong we are and, how much money we make. There's no time left for us, and the result is stress that's rampant and out-of-control.

Stress may be the plague of this society, but you don't have to become caught in the epidemic. While you may not be able to control your surroundings, you certainly can control how life's events affect you.

I hope, with the insight and tools provided in this book, you will gain the self-esteem, confidence and skills you need to beat stress before it beats you.

Now it's time to put this knowledge to the test. I want you to actually see how stressors affect your life and how you react to them. So for the next two weeks, on the following

▼ ▼ ▼

pages, write down all the things—people, places and events—that pull your stress trigger.

Indicate how you reacted to these triggers and evaluate how you could have dealt better with the situation.

After a few entries, you will clearly see how you deal with stress and will be able to cope with these annoyances in a more positive manner in the future. This exercise is an excellent way to put all the information contained in this book to practical use.

For example, let's say the car didn't start and you were already late for work. You blew your top, ranted and raved and worked yourself into a lather.

Write down all these reactions when you have a spare moment, then sit back and plan what you could have done to avoid the stressful situation. Perhaps you should have gotten up a half hour earlier so you would've had more time to deal with such a situation.

You may also mentally note that your temper tantrum did nothing to solve the problem, and decide that next time you'd take a few deep breathes instead of getting angry.

Seeing options in black-and-white will truly help you develop new, stress-busting habits.

In closing, I'd like to share this wonderful poem written by an anonymous author. It appeared in Ann Lander's syndicated column years ago and serves as an example of why we should start living—as human beings—right now.

IF I HAD MY LIFE TO LIVE OVER

Someone asked me the other day, if I had my life to live over, would I change anything? "No," I answered. Then I began to think…

If I had my life to live over, I would have talked less and listened more. I would have invited friends over for dinner

▼ ▼ ▼

even though the carpet was stained and the sofa faded. I would have eaten popcorn in the "good" living room and worried less about dirt when someone wanted to light a fire in the fireplace.

I would have burned the pink candle sculpted like a rose before it melted in storage. I would have sat on the lawn with my children and not worried about grass stains.

I would have cried and laughed less while watching television—and done more of it while watching life. I would have shared more of the responsibilities carried by my wife.

I would have gone to bed when I was sick instead of worrying that the earth would go into a holding pattern if I missed work for one day. I would never buy anything just because it was practical, wouldn't show soil or because it was guaranteed to last a lifetime.

There would have been more "I love you," more "I am sorry"…but mostly, given another shot at life, I would seize every moment, look at it and really see it and live it—and never give it back.

▼ ▼ ▼

▼ ▼ ▼

DAILY STRESS-BUSTING DIARY

WEEK 1

DAY 1

STRESSOR:

_____

_____

_____

_____

_____

_____

MY REACTION:

_____

_____

_____

_____

_____

_____

A BETTER WAY:

_____

_____

_____

_____

_____

_____

_____

▼ ▼ ▼

DAILY STRESS-BUSTING DIARY

WEEK 1

DAY 2

STRESSOR:

_____

_____

_____

_____

_____

_____

_____

MY REACTION:

_____

_____

_____

_____

_____

_____

A BETTER WAY:

_____

_____

_____

_____

_____

_____

▼ ▼ ▼

Daily Stress-Busting Diary

WEEK 1

DAY 3

STRESSOR:

_____

_____

_____

_____

_____

_____

_____

MY REACTION:

_____

_____

_____

_____

_____

_____

_____

A BETTER WAY:

_____

_____

_____

_____

_____

_____

_____

▼ ▼ ▼

DAILY STRESS-BUSTING DIARY

WEEK 1

DAY 4

STRESSOR:

_____

_____

_____

_____

_____

_____

_____

MY REACTION:

_____

_____

_____

_____

_____

_____

_____

A BETTER WAY:

_____

_____

_____

_____

_____

_____

_____

▼ ▼ ▼

DAILY STRESS-BUSTING DIARY

WEEK 1

DAY 5

STRESSOR:

_____

_____

_____

_____

_____

_____

_____

MY REACTION:

_____

_____

_____

_____

_____

_____

_____

A BETTER WAY:

_____

_____

_____

_____

_____

_____

_____

▼ ▼ ▼

DAILY STRESS-BUSTING DIARY

WEEK 1

DAY 6

STRESSOR:

_____

_____

_____

_____

_____

_____

_____

MY REACTION:

_____

_____

_____

_____

_____

_____

_____

A BETTER WAY:

_____

_____

_____

_____

_____

_____

_____

▼ ▼ ▼

DAILY STRESS-BUSTING DIARY

WEEK 1

DAY 7

STRESSOR:

_____

_____

_____

_____

_____

_____

_____

MY REACTION:

_____

_____

_____

_____

_____

_____

_____

A BETTER WAY:

_____

_____

_____

_____

_____

_____

_____

▼ ▼ ▼

DAILY STRESS-BUSTING DIARY

WEEK 2

DAY 1

STRESSOR:

_____
_____
_____
_____
_____
_____
_____

MY REACTION:

_____
_____
_____
_____
_____
_____

A BETTER WAY:

_____
_____
_____
_____
_____
_____

▼ ▼ ▼

DAILY STRESS-BUSTING DIARY

WEEK 2

DAY 2

STRESSOR:

_____

_____

_____

_____

_____

_____

_____

MY REACTION:

_____

_____

_____

_____

_____

_____

A BETTER WAY:

_____

_____

_____

_____

_____

_____

▼ ▼ ▼

DAILY STRESS-BUSTING DIARY

WEEK 2

DAY 3

STRESSOR:

_____

_____

_____

_____

_____

_____

_____

MY REACTION:

_____

_____

_____

_____

_____

_____

_____

A BETTER WAY:

_____

_____

_____

_____

_____

_____

_____

▼ ▼ ▼

DAILY STRESS-BUSTING DIARY

STRESSOR:

_____

_____

_____

_____

_____

_____

_____

MY REACTION:

_____

_____

_____

_____

_____

_____

_____

A BETTER WAY:

_____

_____

_____

_____

_____

_____

_____

▼ ▼ ▼

DAILY STRESS-BUSTING DIARY

WEEK 2

DAY 5

STRESSOR:

_____
_____
_____
_____
_____
_____
_____

MY REACTION:

_____
_____
_____
_____
_____
_____

A BETTER WAY:

_____
_____
_____
_____
_____
_____
_____

▼ ▼ ▼

DAILY STRESS-BUSTING DIARY

WEEK 2

DAY 6

STRESSOR:

_____

_____

_____

_____

_____

_____

MY REACTION:

_____

_____

_____

_____

_____

_____

A BETTER WAY:

_____

_____

_____

_____

_____

_____

▼ ▼ ▼

DAILY STRESS-BUSTING DIARY

WEEK 2

DAY 7

STRESSOR:

_____
_____
_____
_____
_____
_____
_____

MY REACTION:

_____
_____
_____
_____
_____
_____
_____

A BETTER WAY:

_____
_____
_____
_____
_____
_____
_____

▼ ▼ ▼

Index

▼ ▼ ▼

▼ ▼ ▼

▼   ▼   ▼

All COOL HAND titles are available through your local bookstore or by mail. To order directly, return the coupon below to: COOL HAND COMMUNICATIONS, INC., Order Department, 1098 N.W. Boca Raton Blvd., Boca Raton, FL 33432.

New for 1993 (COOL HAND Creations)

How to Cope With Chronic Pain	1-56790-043-7	$9.95	_____
National Park Vacations: The West-Vol. 1	1-56790-012-7	$9.95	_____
Creative Costumes for Children	1-56790-059-3	$11.95	_____
Life & Love in the Paradise Lounge	1-56790-115-8	$6.95	_____
Unfinished Business	1-56790-000-3	$22.95	_____
Lynn Allison Better Lifestyle Series:			
1001 Ways/Life Better	1-56790-097-6	$7.95	_____
The Magic of Garlic	1-56790-098-4	$7.95	_____
Natural Stress-Busters	1-56790-099-2	$7.95	_____
Uncommon Footsteps	1-56790-149-2	$19.95	_____
Hit of the Party	1-56790-063-1	$14.95	_____
World's Worst Cookbook	1-56790-137-9	$8.95	_____

Backlist Beauties (COOL HAND Classics)

Think A Little	1-56790-025-9	$7.95	_____
Compleat Option Player	0-89709-200-7	$14.95	_____
Creative Costumes	1-56790-056-9	$6.95	_____
Dr. Cookie's Cookbook (Comb)	1-56790-109-3	$7.95	_____
Dr. Cookie's Cookbook (Paper)	1-56790-108-5	$6.95	_____
Early American Cookbook	1-56790-087-9	$7.95	_____
Essential Book of Shellfish	1-56790-125-5	$6.95	_____
How to Be a Wine Expert	1-9613525-1-5	$9.95	_____
Muffin Mania	1-56790-074-7	$7.95	_____
One Day Celestial Navigation	1-56790-021-6	$9.95	_____

Sub-total	_____
Please add $2.00 for postage and handling	_____
Florida residents add 6% sales tax to order.	_____
TOTAL	_____

Bill To: _____

_____

_____

_____

Ship To: _____

_____

_____

_____

INC.

A Publishing Company

Don't miss out on these best-selling titles by Lynn Allison!

1001 Ways to Make Your Life Better

Included are quick and easy ways to reduce stress, increase your brain power, improve your family life and take control of your destiny, plus many more. We all want to get our lives organized, maintain our health and stay young at heart. Now we can—simply by opening this book to any page.

The Magic of Garlic

Researchers say garlic wards off cancer and heart disease and keeps the blood healthy by preventing clots; it acts as an antibiotic in fighting colds, and it can even keep fleas off the family dog. *The Magic of Garlic* presents the practical applications of this marvelous herb, along with a historical overview and delicious recipes everyone can use to get more garlic into their daily diets.

Natural Stress-Busters

Stress is a major health problem in this country today, but it is manageable. Lynn Allison reveals how anyone of any age can enjoy a positive, stress-free life by taking advantage of the tools nature has provided for that purpose. In addition to tests to determine stress levels and exercises designed to reduce tension, *Natural Stress-Busters* even includes a two-week diary you can use to measure your progress.

Stress-Busting Meditations

Contains 40 minutes of soothing pre-recorded meditations designed to help you reduce stress and tension. Includes the blissful sounds of nature in the background.

1001 Ways to Make Your Life Better	1-56790-097-6	$7.95	_____
The Magic of Garlic	1-56790-098-4	$7.95	_____
Natural Stress-Busters	1-56790-099-2	$7.95	_____
Stress-Busting Meditations		$9.95	_____
	Sub-total		_____
	Please add $2.00 for postage and handling		_____
	Florida residents add 6.5% sales tax to order.		_____
	TOTAL		_____

Bill To: _____

_____

_____

_____

Ship To: _____

_____

_____

_____